A
Touch of Glory

Also by Alun Richards

Novels

THE ELEPHANT YOU GAVE ME
THE HOME PATCH
A WOMAN OF EXPERIENCE
HOME TO AN EMPTY HOUSE
ENNAL'S POINT
BARQUE WHISPER

Short Story Collections

DAI COUNTRY
THE FORMER MISS MERTHYR TYDFIL

Plays

THE BIG BREAKER
THE VICTUALLERS' BALL
THE SNOWDROPPER
THE HORIZONTAL LIFE

Television Plays

GOING LIKE A FOX
O CAPTAIN, MY CAPTAIN
NOTHING TO PAY
HEAR THE TIGER, SEE THE BAY
THE HOT POTATO BOYS
READY FOR THE GLORY
TAFFY CAME TO MY HOUSE
WHO STEALS MY NAME
ALBINOS IN BLACK
THE STRAIGHT AND NARROW
THE PRINCELY GIFT
HARRY LIFTERS

Television Adaptations

THE SCHOOLMASTER (SIMENON)
VESSEL OF WRATH (W. SOMERSET MAUGHAM)
LOVE AND MR LEWISHAM (H. G. WELLS)
ACTING CAPTAIN (ALUN LEWIS)

(as Editor)

THE PENGUIN BOOK OF WELSH SHORT STORIES
THE PENGUIN BOOK OF SEA STORIES
AGAINST THE WAVES

A Touch of Glory

100 YEARS OF WELSH RUGBY

Alun Richards

LONDON
MICHAEL JOSEPH

First published in Great Britain by
Michael Joseph Ltd.,
44 Bedford Square, London WC1
1980

ISBN 0 7181 1938 X

Filmset and printed in Great Britain by
BAS Printers Limited, Over Wallop, Hampshire.
Bound by Hunter and Foulis, Edinburgh

Contents

List of Illustrations

page

Acknowledgements

During my research for BBC Wales' Centenary Film, I was privileged to talk to a large number of distinguished old players and journalists as well as the official historians of the Welsh Rugby Union, Dr David Smith and Mr Gareth Williams. I would like to thank them, Mr Carwyn James who contributes his own expertise in a concluding afterword, and all those who allowed me the opportunity of seeing their scrapbooks, mementoes and private book collections; in particular, Cliff Jones Esq., O.B.E., M.A., President of the Welsh Rugby Union, Mr J. B. G. Thomas, Sports Editor of the *Western Mail*, Mr John Morris, Mr A. Gould and Mr W. H. Travers. To the producers of the film, Mr Onllwyn Brace, Sports Organiser for BBC Wales, Mr Ray Williams, Centenary Officer of the W.R.U., and its director, Mr Chris Lawrence, I also owe my thanks. A full acknowledgement to the photographers is contained elsewhere, but my especial thanks are due to Mr John Harris, Mr Ronnie Thomas, formerly Chief Staff Photographer of the *South Wales Evening Post*, and also to Mr Fred Croster, Editor of *Welsh Rugby Magazine*, and to BBC Wales.

There are also a number of indispensable books on Welsh rugby football to which I owe a debt of gratitude, principally: John Billot's *History of Welsh International Rugby*; J. B. G. Thomas's *The Men in Scarlet*; *Rugby Recollections* by W. J. T. Collins, as well as the histories and brochures of the famous clubs and the daily reports of many correspondents in newspapers ranging from the *Cambrian* to the *Western Mail* whose coverage of the game in Wales is in every way an expression of our intense interest. But above all, my debt is to the players, past and present, capped and uncapped, whose own enjoyment has never ceased to be mine.

Alun Richards

'More than any other nation we have invented the cult of the famous player.' Cliff Jones (Cardiff, Cambridge University and Wales), a classic fly-half, now President of the Welsh Rugby Union.

I

In the Beginning

This essay is not intended to be a history of Welsh rugby football but an attempt to explain some of its attributes, written to celebrate a hundredth birthday and including the memoirs and imaginings of a fan—as harmless and as deadly as that! Prejudices and inconsistencies will no doubt pepper the text, and since the Welsh have always had a predilection for litigation, I shall have to be on my guard. No one man, in my view, can explain the totality of his own people or their national game, and since Wales is severely divided between north and south by a mass of sparsely populated highlands with hardly a set of rugby posts in sight, I had better explain that I am very much a South Walian, non-Welsh-speaking—we have two tongues—with my face ever turned towards the sea.

It is always important in Wales to explain where you hail from, for at any given time there are likely assailants lurking around every corner, ever ready to demonstrate that you might not be 'really Welsh', or that whatever you happen to be doing, you probably have no business to be doing it. We breed critics like mayfly in permanent hatch. No Welsh boxer, poet, footballer, athlete or dramatist has ever suffered worse in the metropolitan capitals of the world than he has done at home. In every street there are tumbrils already waiting for the newly born and very often ambition is a *risqué* word. 'Watch it, boy!' the very terraced houses seem to be saying at times, or, 'Who do you think you are?'

The critics are great levellers and the wits come out like flowers after the rain. Act in some way above your local expectation and you are likely to find your appearance and character dismissed very cryptically—'Fur coat and no knickers!'

The habit of giving nicknames, necessary because of common surnames like Jones or Davies, remains to this day, and as I write a rural county council, finding it necessary to appoint a shepherd to keep straying sheep from a new motorway have landed a young employee with the nickname Dai Bo Peep. Sheep as well as rugby players roam all over Wales. In the Rhondda they visit the cinema and feed out of dustbins, and there are performers still alive who remember the old Tonypandy Empire when music-hall acts were interrupted by them.

What, you may ask, has any of this got to do with rugby football?

Simply that, in my view, we have brought to our national game many aspects of our varied selves and our turbulent history which are set against the grey terrain where so many of us live. We have also brought our dreams to play a part in the Saturday drama that, on occasions, becomes the theatre of our lives. We identify with our national teams more completely than any other nation in the United Kingdom, but more than that, in our rugby football we yearn for some expression of ourselves, always hoping for that ecstasy which comes from a glimpse of some denied part of our private lives. We also tend to go through the full circle of our emotions very quickly. When we are up, as others have observed, we are very up, and when we are down, we are almost out of sight. We also ask for too much, and now and again we get it.

And there is also another point to be included in the case notes. Such

'When we are down, we are almost out of sight'—Phil Bennett offers consolation, Llanelli v. Bridgend, 1979

is our passion that some of us are not quite right, three ha'pence short of a shilling where rugby football is concerned. Not only are most of us guilty of the most fiercely partisan loyalties, but sometimes, in our veneration for one particular player, we become blind to the attributes of his rivals. There are also—and there always have been—fierce divisions between the eastern and western rugby-playing areas of Wales which have the same blinkering effect. If each town had a diplomatic corps, we would be breaking off diplomatic relations every other season; and, although many of us would deny it, the pleasures of playing English clubs, or special clubs like the London Welsh which have brought a new style and *élan* to our game are often greater than the

'Sometimes we are not quite right!' A heated exchange, Llanelli v. Bridgend, 1978 bloodstained local derbies which still occur.

Then there are the mythology, the jokes, the wisecracks, and the apocryphal tales which tell of lives being altered because of some rugby occasion. Our obsession is force-fed at times by the attention given to it by the media and now advertisers who have cottoned on to a long period of recent success. Some of our best-known players now and again peer at us from the newspapers as they advertise this building society or that, and you are quite likely to find a former superstar modelling clothes or opening a supermarket, or inviting you to purchase his life story. Alternatively you might be entering his restaurant or buying the products he represents. There is scarcely a supporter who has not got some revealing tale to tell about one or other of the recent 'greats'. Perhaps the choicest tale concerns the remark

From early days to the present, players have always attracted the attention of advertisers, whether their products be a smoke, a chew, a good listen, or a nice drop of *Perrier-Jouët* from the player of the year.

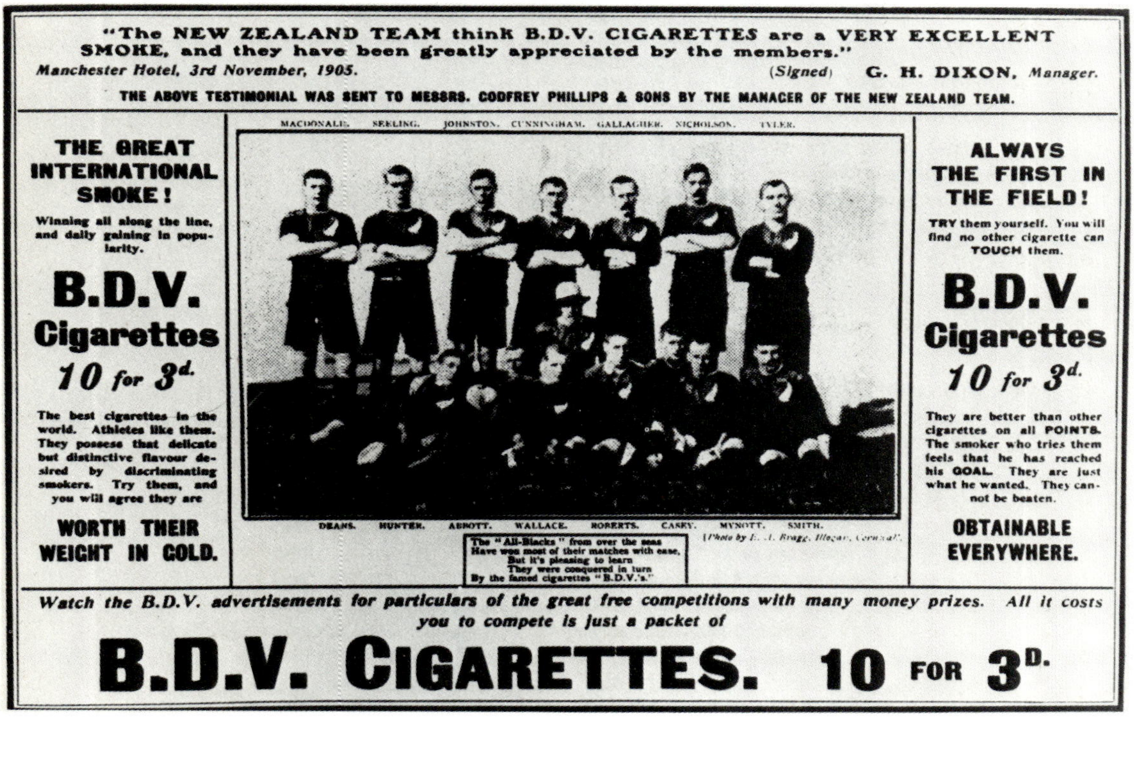

DAN JONES,
ABERAVON
T. E. JONES AND Co

WALES v ENGLAND
RUGBY
INTERNATIONAL
REDIFFUSION
YOUR GRAND STAND SEAT
for PERFECT LISTENING
WALES v ENGLAND
REDIFFUSION
WALES v ENGLAND
REDIFFUSION

C. BRICE,
ABERAVON
T. E. JONES AND Co

Gareth Edwards signing copies of his autobiography at Selfridges.

overheard by Gareth Edwards' mother who had the misfortune to break her leg at a time of heavy snow in her native village of Gwauncaegurwen. It took some time for the ambulance to arrive, and when she was finally lying on a stretcher inside she could not help overhearing a relieved well-wisher saying, 'There's one thing anyway—it could have been Gareth!'

Such tales are legion. If it had not occurred, it would have been invented, and the stories have travelled around with Welshmen who have made the game known for what it is, a national obsession. In Italy, where we have exported coaches and players, you are quite likely to hear—as I did recently—an irate Welsh coach shouting, 'Avanti! Avanti!' from the touchline, and then swearing in Welsh the next minute. But more importantly, players like Bernard Thomas of Llanelli or Robin Williams of Pontypool have left an elegant and stylish impression of Welsh play upon the Italians and forged links which would not otherwise have been made. We tend to disapprove of players who migrate but coaches are another matter, and no doubt when Carwyn James, the most famous and articulate of Welsh coaches, took

Bernard Thomas of Llanelli and Aberavon

'They tell me it's a very rough game.' Tactical or spiritual guidance for Carwyn James?

his Italian championship team to meet the Pope, as is the custom, back home in Cefneithin they thought it no more than right. The process is a neat reversal of the old Welsh temperance syndrome (drink—debt—ruin—the gutter!), with prowess at rugby football leading to sainthood or deification, and there is no doubt that any Welshman's success in the game is somehow a success shared by the privileged but ever expanding few who knew him intimately when young. We are very much people of place: each place has its hero and each hero a particular deed or style which is associated with him and can somehow never be taken away from him. It might be the superb athleticism of a Gareth Edwards break around the scrum, the elusive jinking run of Gerald Davies in full flight, J. P. R. Williams on a sudden burst, the insolent coolness of Barry John with his computer kicking; or we might store other memory pictures of the hard men of Welsh packs—the dour, inscrutable countenance of Graham Price, the implacable stare of Brian Thomas, the sheer physical bulk of Geoff Wheel, the merest glimpse of the flying wings from J. J. Williams to Maurice Richards or Ken Jones or Dewi Bebb who remain in the mind for sheer pace. Then again, there are the famous tries and the moves that led to them. These have a special significance since we very often recall the whole movement from the time the ball was won; then, if we think of line-out jumpers, we come back down the memory train from Alan Martin through Delme Thomas to Roy John and John Gwilliam, who brought a more sophisticated ball-winning technique to the post-war decade. Naturally, we also remember incidents or

left, J. P. R. Williams, always the attacker who scorned convention

right, Gareth Edwards, one of the greatest ever Welsh half-backs, making a dive pass

above, Barry John
right, Gerald Davies

Opposite page: above, The celebrated Pontypool front row, Graham Price, Bobby Windsor and 'Charlie' Faulkner
below, left and right, 'Rugby football is a game for those who can play pianos as well as those who can shift them.' Geoff Wheel of Swansea in duet.

MORRIS & THOMAS

Opposite page: above, Maurice Richards scoring the fourth of his tries against England in 1969

below, left and right, The flying wings, John Bevan and J. J. Williams

above and right, Ken Jones and Dewi Bebb, two more flying wings

Just as we remember famous players, so do we recall famous occasions. Perhaps it is a try that remains forever in the memory.

Terry Davies (Llanelli) scoring the solitary try of a club game against Neath

offenders and victims which remain often unfairly in the memory since one incident should never categorise a great player. But most of all we remember success, and while the fickleness of crowds is probably not much different in any sport, Welsh rugby probably remains more closely tied to a rugby-playing populace than does soccer or cricket. There are reasons why this should be so, but they do not fully explain the total amount of time we spend thinking or talking about the game, nor why most of us have at one time or another played imaginary games when we pick the greatest sides ever. If we have not picked ourselves we recall the players who have most impressed us and then speak emphatically about them as if they were still playing. My own theory is that if you have the luck to see the great players in the formative years of your life, they are likely to burn themselves on the consciousness, creating an impression so fiercely and brilliantly etched that no others can quite replace them. It is so in my own case, and I hasten to say once more that this essay is not written from the point of view of the expert but by one who takes his accustomed stance on the terrace, likes to savour what he sees, but reserves the right if things are not going well to substitute for present players those of the past. Any man can dream and today's players—the most filmed, photographed and publicised in the history of the game—must take their places against others, including those described on the hearsay evidence of those who have passed into limbo. One of the tragedies of rugby football as an art form—which I believe it sometimes is—is that so much of it can only exist in the memory and it needs an act of the imagination to remind us of this.

I mean, very simply, that we are, in regard to so much of the past,

Keith Jarrett converting in a dream début for Wales against England in 1967. Aged 18, playing full back for the first time, he scored 19 points to equal the record of W. J. Bancroft established in 1910.

The end of the match between Wales and Fiji in September 1964, the most joyous game of the decade when the Fijians reminded us that rugby was a handling and running game.

similar to music lovers who can only talk about a great musician's performances because they have been destroyed with him. They only exist in the memory of those who have heard them, and their memory can thus only be enjoyed by an act of the imagination. In a hundred years' time great players like Gareth Edwards or Gerald Davies will be compared with their successors because they will exist on film, but no one will be able to make the same comparisons with players of whom we have no living memory. We are thus handicapped unless we can dream, and yet, when we use such phrases as 'a classic fly-half', we are implying that we have a notion of style which extends into a past we have never seen. All these are matters to touch upon, particularly in the case of Welsh half-backs.

I have mentioned critics but I believe it is important to ignore them.

At the other end of the emotional scale, the giving end, the nation rises in vociferous empathy with a fierce and burning pride of possession for those special individuals who have shaken off the constraints of anonymity and then triumphed on a global scale. Nowhere is this more obvious than in sporting fields and it is no surprise to me that the universal regard in which a sporting protagonist is held is very often matched by extraordinary achievement. Having passed the first barriers the world opens up, as it were. No heat is more fierce than the flames flickering from forked tongues around the corner of the chapel, the public house or the Workmen's Hall, and when I tell you that no fewer than three boxing champions come from a five-mile radius of my home town of Pontypridd, I do so with that pride of place which characterises more races than the Welsh. But there they are: Tom Thomas, Freddie Welsh and Jimmy Wilde, the last two still included in *Ring Magazine*'s rating of *All Time Greats*, a singular distinction. I shall come to the rugby champions later, but for me, the picture of these poor men's sons,

Boxing champions: *left*, Freddie Welsh, Tom Thomas and Jim Driscoll, and *right*, Jimmy Wilde. 'The success of Welsh boxers, many of them world champions, was a stiffener to morale in a society which had been turned upside down by the coal rush.'

hungry fighters from the Welsh valleys and ports, has always been a part of the immediate Welsh past and more meaningful than the Welshmen of legend like Owain Glyndwr, the last king of Wales who lived by fire and the sword. Patriots who are remembered in the purely Welsh sense today usually have to do with the Welsh language, spoken now by a minority of Wales' two-and-a-half million people, but I join common cause with the men on the terraces and salute the more popular heroes who have taken the world as their stage.

Wales, it cannot be said often enough, is very small. You can drive across it in any direction in one day. The bulk of its population live in one highly concentrated industrial area forming the counties of Glamorgan and Monmouthshire, but its famous sons are drawn from every county. I have mentioned boxers since in one sense they were the first to blaze the modern trail of taking Welsh sporting talent to the world, but also because they were part of that same industrial society which fermented and created modern Wales. I do not believe that there is an actual connection between boxing and rugby football in the sporting sense—although some hard-done-by opponents might believe so!—but the success of our boxers in the greater world occurred at a time when Welshmen very probably had doubts about themselves. The creation of champions who could take on all-comers was a stiffener to morale in a society which had been turned upside down by the coal rush between 1871 and 1911 when the population of Wales increased by almost a million. The increase, as is well known, was preceded by internal migration in Wales with people leaving the countryside to come to the towns and mining valleys of Glamorgan and Monmouthshire, but there were also migrants from elsewhere, the West Country in particular. What did they find just before the turn of the century? They were changing cottages for terraces, rural space and village life for the crowded shoulder-to-shoulder empathy of pit-bonded men who now increasingly began to work in one industry alone. If they did not travel far in geographical terms, they certainly did in terms of time, for the modern world exploded around them. In Merthyr, the first Welsh urban experience of any size, they found in Dr David Smith's words:

> a higgledy-piggledy riot of buildings and architectural styles strung out along valleys and places that were, in any normal sense, topographically lunatic. But this was not a normal place. Here public houses were built of a gargantuan dimension which implied that the thirst for soporific was insatiable whilst chapels were thrown up as if they were going out of fashion—and they did. Where there had been silence, there was a cacophonous noise; where there had been relative immobility, there was now an intricate network of railway lines mocking landscape problems with arching viaducts and looming grey stone embankment walls around which basic convenience roads and streets were constructed. In the high street, yawning emporia offered the flotsam and jetsam washed up by the industrial economy, ready-made clothes and boots, convenience foods, tawdry goods and ornaments, entertainment in music-hall and boxing booths, milk deliveries and newspapers and magazines. This society had the stumbling vitality of a blind man on a spree.*

It is this vitality which had to wait years for its expression in sporting terms. First the boxers and world champion cyclists like Jimmy Michael of Aberdare, who beat all-comers in long distance rides all over the USA, and then, slowly at first, it found expression in the English game which was brought here from the public schools of England. Does any of this, I can hear some people asking still, have anything at all to do with rugby football in Wales now? My answer is yes, it does, just as I believe with others that the development of the will-of-the-wisp Welsh half-back, the darting idol of the crowds who has dominated Welsh rugby football since the game began, is also related both to the steep terrain of the mountain valleys and to the very expectations of the crowd.

In Wales, rugby fans are more like participating audiences than crowds and at times they have steaming expectations. Their collective will is all-powerful. Sometimes they are well-behaved and knowledgeable,

*Dr David Smith, 'Wales Through the Looking Glass' Lecture to *Yr Academi Cymraeg*, 1978.

Faces in the crowd—'we breed critics like mayfly in permanent hatch'

sometimes they are not, but always they are there, making a sixteenth man on the great occasions, and it is incredible to think that when the game started they were absent, for it was first developed in the public schools amongst an élite who had been separated from their fellows. The passage of person and interest from the independent 'private' schools to the public parks which followed was unique in Wales and remains the great contribution of the Welsh to the game. This transference did not happen as quickly elsewhere in Britain although the closest parallel must have been in a similar kind of developing industrial society in Yorkshire and Lancashire. There the game was all too soon to be hived off into a separate union when England lost some of its strongest clubs after the famous dispute over the payment of

'Few escape the fervour . . .

players to compensate for time lost from their employment.

But this is old stuff. What interests me is how the game spread in Wales. On the one hand, schools like Llandovery College, Lampeter College and Christ's College, Brecon, with masters on their staffs who had been to Rugby School or the English universities where the game was also played, were obviously in receipt of the codified rules which were the necessary blueprint. Old Rugbeians or old Malburians had their ready-made Welsh counterparts and almost all the major Welsh clubs were formed by old boys who were the sons of the emerging Welsh middle class, although they might not necessarily be Welsh in origin. The Cheltenham College Rules with twenty players a side, 'and the ball never to be picked up unless "dapped"', provided the code for

. . . although visitors may opt out'

the first games in Merthyr and Cardiff and it is clear that the old boy influence was the most important. We know that the occupations of these first players represent an emerging professional class in a busy, prosperous and expanding society, and the doctors, lawyers, engineers, surveyors and brewers were probably little different from their English and Scottish counterparts except that, by necessity, they were crowded together in the two most populous counties of Wales. Scotsmen were prominent from the outset, bringing from the Scottish public schools the same knowledge of the game. Dr T. P. Whittington, Neath's first international and founder of the club (with seven solicitors!) played for Scotland against England at the Oval seven years before Wales entered the international arena. In the same club a Dr E. V. Pegge, a Welsh international whose father kept the last private lunatic asylum in Wales, once chartered a special train to catch up with his team-mates when they had left on a special tour of Devon. It was the same Dr Pegge

Dr E. V. Pegge

'Short shorts, old man?'

(whose sister married Sir George White, the defender of Ladysmith) who created a sensation by playing with arms and legs bare, disapproving of the shin-length knicker-bocker and successfully moving at the first club meeting 'that baths be provided forthwith and that the secretary be instructed to obtain prices for same'.

The young men of these clubs knew exactly what kind of game they wanted to play and one can imagine the confidence, style and assurance which they brought to their Saturday outings. The history of the famous Cardiff club records: 'There was no regulation costume worn then; most of the players turning out in ordinary attire, just taking off their coats, one player even playing on one occasion in evening dress, and some did not discard their bowler hats.'

The first game which the same history notes was with Cowbridge Grammar School against the Glamorgan Football Club in 1874, 'the team journeying to Cowbridge in a coach and four'. On the return, one of the players displaced the driver, a turnpike gate was broken and a lamp-post badly damaged, the cost of repair being met by a hastily organized concert. Cardiff had a number of clubs which ultimately amalgamated because they were easily beaten by representative teams from Newport and Swansea.

From the beginning, with champagne corks popping at that organised concert, it was clear that the new game for the new society had a social cachet about it and very little in common with the traditional Welsh games like knappan and bando or the old Roman squash ball games like harpastum. However, the *Western Mail* of 1896 included the story of a match which took place at Llandysul in 1719.

Football in 1719. All Day Match at Llandysul

A correspondent writes—In view of the popularity of Football nowadays, the following description of a game played on Christmas Day 1719 may be of interest to your readers. The Teams consisted of players from the parishes of Llanwenog (Carms) and Llandysul (Cards) and the description is contained in a letter written by a young lady, of which the following is a fairly literal translation:

They had been preparing for months, and hundreds had assembled to witness the game. I went there in spite of my father's wish, but my brother Jenkin stayed at home in consequence of my father's threats. Many persons had brewed up for the occasion and had taken with them to the field food and drink, and lo what running, kicking, noise and shouting there were there. Now one side won, and then the other, but Llandysul was the more frequent victor.

The play was suspended for an hour at mid-day for the players to partake of bread, cheese and beer and all were as merry as the cuckoo. Soon after resuming play in the afternoon, the members of the Teams began to fall out and curse and kick one another. Some were drunk, others had drunk heavily and they, after beating each other, presented a terrible sight, the Maids running and screaming in their endeavours to save their brothers and friends, but, in spite of their

> efforts, the men continued to fight like bulldogs—I should think they fought for an hour when the Llanwenog men were forced to retreat.
>
> Evan Bwlchgwyn was far too gone in drink to defend himself and would have been half killed had not his sister and myself dragged him away. It was said that one of the Llanwenog boys had been killed, he was unconscious for a time, but after a while came to himself and is now recovered. Tom Penddol was somewhat badly kicked as he was too drunk to take care of himself. The conflict is much talked about elsewhere and the two Parishes threaten to renew hostilities with cudgels sometime in the summer. The Llanwenog boys are reputed to be doughty wielders of cudgels. Sally Blaenycwm gave one of the Llanwenog boys a thorough licking; she struck him with her fist repeatedly and the blood spurted at every stroke.
>
> Mr Lewis, the Minister, spoke severely of the occurrence at Pantycreuddyn afterwards, and cried like a baby, and my father and my mother and all the old people cried. They have been holding meetings several times since to pray for the young people, but I do not observe that the young people are a whit better after having been prayed for.

Later, when whole communities became involved, the same fierce partisan loyalties were to reassert themselves. 'They contend not', wrote George Owen describing players of the ancient mob football in Pembrokeshire in 1603, 'for any wager or valuable thing, but strive to the death for glory and fame which they esteem dearer than any wordly wealth.' Glory was thus ever present and while mob football or bando (played with sticks) might have enthused the locals, they were blood sports compared to the public school game.

From the beginning, in the 1860s and '70s, the dominant influences in the formation of the Welsh clubs were persons of wealth and substance, representatives of the landed families who very frequently contributed towards the provision of the grounds. Then there were the new servants of the industrialists, the professional men who had taken up residence, all of them contributing to what was to become a booming and vibrant economy.

In the years between 1870 and 1900, however, rugby football suddenly became a mass spectator sport in Wales. There was probably little difference between the old boys' clubs of provincial England and Wales up to the founding of the South Wales Football Club in 1875, but the terrain was different and the South Wales towns and valleys were growing apace. Being situated quite near to each other with the railways developing at the same time, communications became easier. Not only was South Wales opened up to itself but it was opened up to England as well, and from the very first seasons there were visits by the

The Victorian South Wales which saw the birth of the South Wales game was 'a higgledy-piggledy riot of buildings and architectural styles strung out in valleys and places that were topographically lunatic'.

Sandbrook's showrooms in Merthyr

above left, Pontypridd in 1900
above right, Pentre landslide
centre, 3 public houses in Aberdare
below, Trinity Methodist Chapel, Aberdare

major clubs like Cardiff, Swansea, Newport and Llanelli to play against English clubs where they very soon became star attractions, welcome for their style of play and their effect on gate money. Newport in their second season played Edgbaston Crusaders at Birmingham as well as Rocklease at Clifton, but several years later were trounced by Blackheath by four goals eight tries to nil, a shattering defeat from which 'much was learned'. Cardiff soon had fixtures with Moseley Harriers and Swansea were playing Wakefield Trinity and Huddersfield by the 1880s.

But first things first. I like to think that there were a number of factors which led to the opening up of an exclusive game to the whole populace in Wales. First, there was the dynamic of the new society with new jobs for new people, when social mobility was at its height; and amidst the great movement of persons and the growth of towns there was, perhaps for the first time in Welsh society, a readiness to mix and a welcome for change which was dictated by the world demand for coal and the new industries which sprang up with coal at the fountainhead. It is not surprising that the clubs were often called by the industries which dominated the towns. Llanelli were called the Tin-Platers, Swansea the Metallurgists, and although at first the players were neither tin-platers nor metallurgists, they would soon be drawn from amongst those who had a direct physical connection with these industries, which was to prove important. People had come into the towns and the ports from the countryside and, having made the journey, they had opened up new vistas for themselves.

My grandfather, a blacksmith's son from the Carmarthenshire village of Conwyl Elvet, remembered doffing his cap as a boy of twelve to Lord Dynevor, the local proprietor of great landed estates. He had left school at twelve, grateful to get a start in life as a grocer's boy in Carmarthen. One can imagine that he grew up in an almost feudal tradition that had been unchanged for centuries. When he soon afterwards found employment with the expanding chain of stores run by Tommy Lipton, a new horizon opened up for him and he actually travelled as far as Edinburgh, eventually making his way as a young manager to Pontypridd at the foot of the Rhondda valley. There he met my grandmother whose own family had lived and farmed in the area for generations. His journey in life was fortunate in the sense that he did not suffer physically from the ills of the coal face like hundreds of his contemporaries who came directly from the farms to the pits. Yet he travelled the same road in terms of geography and was witness to the growth of towns like Pontypridd, whose inhabitants were a healthy mixture of old stock and newcomers from the Welsh countryside and from across the Bristol Channel. The latter brought with them the names of remote Devon and Somerset villages which were to puzzle me in the obituaries I read as a child.

It was this mix of all-comers from which rugby football was to find its most profitable feeding ground, and it was no accident, in my view, that a new game was to draw strength from new people who had already begun to assume a new identity. It offered them status and a sense of belonging. My grandfather would not have liked the description 'new people' since he maintained his connection with the Welsh language and the chapel all his life. Nevertheless, the people with whom he did business were drawn from varied backgrounds, and his own children grew up differently; for the Welsh language came to be associated with rural attitudes and had no part to play in the world in which they lived or aspired to. But while this old Wales with its strict Nonconformist mores was to linger on well into the next century, the change had already begun and it is interesting that the newly-formed rugby clubs were to think of themselves as South Walian, rather than Welsh, and one of the first concerns was that their game should be thought of as on a par with that of the English clubs.

Many club players at this time had dual qualifications; some of them, it should be said, were wholly English like Frank Hancock, the Somersetshire brewer who came to Cardiff at the age of twenty-one and was instrumental in founding the four three-quarter system, or Gwyn Nicholls, the great Welsh centre who was born in Westbury-on-Severn. It was, of course, the most natural thing in the world that they should first want to establish themselves as equals with those who had taught them the game, in exactly the same way as New Zealanders or

South Africans did overseas. Parity was not possible, one suspects, simply because the number of ex-public schoolboys and university men who were domiciled in South Wales was considerably less than in England, and so the game was soon opened up to a broader section of society in the towns where the first clubs were formed, this lessening of exclusivity being further encouraged when fierce local rivalry developed.

There was also another requirement, built into the nature of the game itself, when it was seen that a wide variety of physical types was needed. It is a little too simple to say that rugby football is a game for those who can play pianos and those who can shift them, but once a division of labour had been established between mauling, passing and hacking it was clear that there would be long periods of the game when there was no question of anyone handling the ball. There was a definite demand for big, strong men who could shove, leaving others to move like chessmen, and it so happened that the new society had a very special

The Hancocks of Cardiff. Frank was the instigator of the four three-quarter system, a Welsh contribution to the game.

'From the pits, the docks and the foundries, feet were hurrying, burlier arms and rougher hands were outstretched to give and take in a game which offered a place for a wide variety of physical types.

need for muscle. This was not by any means the whole story, and Welsh rugby football was not famed for its piano shifters in the early stages, but in the beginning the presence of a rough and tumble society provided burly recruits and artful dodgers and this was crucial. The piano players and piano shifters were to be drawn from every part of this society and some of the most ingenious chords in the rugby sonata were struck by men from the most humble circumstances. This in turn led to the fusion between crowd and player which came to be a feature of games played in Wales. Heroes appeared and soon there developed the cult of the famous player, ever the distinctive feature of Welsh rugby. When the game passed from the private schools to the public parks, so also did it cease to be merely a game because it then became a kind of theatre for the people who watched it.

It is not difficult to imagine the craving for Saturdays felt by the miners and others who made up the crowds. Many of them had jobs which did not lead to an identifiable finished product. What they produced, they saw streaming away in a never-ending shuffle of railway trucks to the ports. The fruits of their daily labour were not to be admired permanently as standing monuments to their sweat and skill. The harvest was hewn or forged and then trundled away, leaving more empty spaces to be filled. Outside their place of work, there was the chapel, the choir and the local eisteddfodau, it was true, but it was on the park where all could meet, where all could triumph, where Jack was as good as his master, and where, for a few coppers, you could see your heroes demonstrate those skills which some of them were to demonstrate like performers, not players. No doubt this led to complications, for if the game was already ceasing to be only a game in the eyes of its most passionate supporters, it must very soon have created problems for its well-known players as they were made aware that they carried responsibilities which belied the idea of rugby football as a game to be played for its own sake, or a team exercise to help you keep fit, or a relaxation from work. The genial conviviality of old boys getting together for a Saturday reunion which was to typify so much of English rugby football was thus soon a thing of the past for some players in Wales, as it was in those areas of England where the game was opened up to all social classes. The difference between amateurism and professionalism was not simply a matter of money but of attitude from the very start, and one suspects that losers were a poor investment in terms of gate money or civic ego. Of course, there were easy matches, but at its most fierce Welsh club rugby, with a challenge cup to be won from its earliest days, was fraught with challenge and responsibility. Out of this pressure came a third factor which was to make our game more of a loaded cocktail than that of our neighbours.

First, a new social mobility brought with it a new game for new players; secondly, because the game offered rewards for a wide variety of physical types, it implied a more robust social mix; and thirdly, within a decade we were in search of heroes, men for whom the touchlines were not so much touchlines as footlights. It was as if, shaken

'Sometimes we expect to see performers, not players, foot-lights instead of touchlines.' Steve Fenwick waits.

Albert Jenkins (Llanelli and Wales)—by common consent, one of the greatest centre three-quarters of all time. The timing of his passes was reported as being the best of any centre, save Bleddyn Williams, of the post-war decade.

by the social upheaval which changed the very landscape of our towns and villages, we needed evidence that we were not as ordinary as the machines seemed intent upon making us, so that we created heroes as we needed them. From this early period in the last thirty years of the nineteenth century, we began the cult of the famous player which has remained a feature of Welsh rugby football throughout the hundred years of the Union. Even in the height of the industrial depression which was to follow the first war, men like Albert Jenkins or Cliff Jones of W. T. H. Davies were to capture the newspaper headlines and become the most discussed Welshmen of their day, a process that was begun soon after the first representative sides were formed.

Richard Mullock, the first secretary of the Welsh Rugby Union, and the first to organise an international match against England in 1881.

The motive for picking such representative sides was undoubtedly to challenge the stronger sides of England. The South Wales Football Club was formed after a meeting in the Castle Hotel in Brecon in 1875. Several years later, the South Wales Football Union—with black jersey and white leek—had as one of its most energetic members one Richard Mullock, a Newport printer who later became the first secretary of the Welsh Rugby Union. He remains a man of mystery, but there is no doubt that his part in the administration of the game was crucial in the early years. As secretary of the Newport Club, he was used to success. Newport had had four invincible seasons between 1874 and 1878 and it was Richard Mullock who arranged a team to play England on Mr

Richardson's field at Blackheath in February 1881. This followed a meeting at the Tenby Hotel in Swansea in March 1880 when clubs represented were Cardiff, Chepstow, Haverfordwest, Llandaff, Llanelli, Neath, Newport, Pontypridd and Swansea. The decision to change the leek emblem for the Prince of Wales' feathers had been made much earlier and they were first worn by the Welsh side in 1888. No doubt the royal emblem was substituted to add a dimension of respectability.

At this time, Welsh club football had already become competitive. Excursion trains were run, there were fierce partisan loyalties and ferocious inter-town loyalties when local newspapers did not hesitate to chastise their rivals. After a cup final match between Llanelli and Cardiff at the time, a correspondent in the *Llanelli Guardian* reported in no uncertain terms: 'The question is not one of merely beating fifteen men . . . it means much more. It means vindicating the honour of Llanelli against many detractors, the editor of the *South Wales Daily News* included. It means raising a name and fame among the towns. . . .' When a Dewsbury team from the North of England played Neath, the same newspaper commented, 'Their reception at Neath signified a striking contrast to what they had experienced at Llanelli. The Neath players were exceedingly disagreeable to them and the few spectators who were present, except for a few Llanellites, conducted themselves as they usually do.' Swansea, a nearer rival, was described disapprovingly as being 'richly endowed with well-dressed rowdies', a criticism that was frequently made on other occasions, and with these attitudes prevailing it is not hard to imagine the uproar which prevailed when the first-ever Welsh team ran off the field at Blackheath in February 1881, having lost by seven goals, one dropped goal and six tries to nil!

Said *The Field*, 'Looked at from whatever point of view, it is impossible to congratulate the Welsh Rugby Union team on their first match with England, unless it were on their pluck in coming so far with the prospect of almost certain defeat.'

Immediate allegations of skulduggery followed. Was this Mr Mullock's private team? A member of the team, the Rev. E. Peake

(Malborough School and Oxford University), who also played for Chepstow, has said that a trial match was held in Swansea before the team was selected, but the general opinion was that Mullock had blundered by picking a team that was unrepresentative of West Wales. The same allegations were made following the establishment of a Welsh Football Association in Ruabon in North Wales when a team to play Scotland was raised in 1876, and in fact Wales did not score a goal until four years later. Blunder or not, it is significant that when the Welsh Rugby Union proper was formed at a meeting in the Castle Hotel, Neath, on 12 March 1881, Mullock was appointed Secretary. In

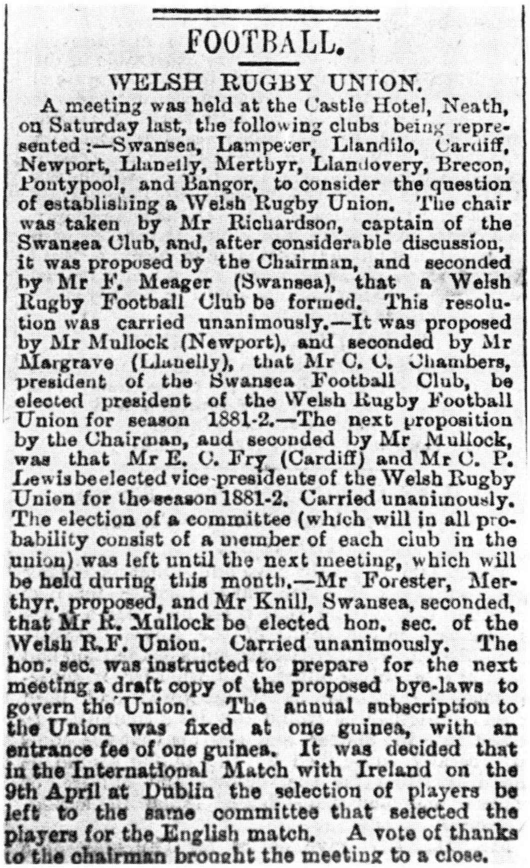

FOOTBALL.

WELSH RUGBY UNION.

A meeting was held at the Castle Hotel, Neath, on Saturday last, the following clubs being represented:—Swansea, Lampeter, Llandilo, Cardiff, Newport, Llanelly, Merthyr, Llandovery, Brecon, Pontypool, and Bangor, to consider the question of establishing a Welsh Rugby Union. The chair was taken by Mr Richardson, captain of the Swansea Club, and, after considerable discussion, it was proposed by the Chairman, and seconded by Mr F. Meager (Swansea), that a Welsh Rugby Football Club be formed. This resolution was carried unanimously.—It was proposed by Mr Mullock (Newport), and seconded by Mr Margrave (Llanelly), that Mr C. C. Chambers, president of the Swansea Football Club, be elected president of the Welsh Rugby Football Union for season 1881-2.—The next proposition by the Chairman, and seconded by Mr Mullock, was that Mr E. C. Fry (Cardiff) and Mr C. P. Lewis be elected vice-presidents of the Welsh Rugby Union for the season 1881-2. Carried unanimously. The election of a committee (which will in all probability consist of a member of each club in the union) was left until the next meeting, which will be held during this month.—Mr Forester, Merthyr, proposed, and Mr Knill, Swansea, seconded, that Mr R. Mullock be elected hon. sec. of the Welsh R.F. Union. Carried unanimously. The hon. sec. was instructed to prepare for the next meeting a draft copy of the proposed bye-laws to govern the Union. The annual subscription to the Union was fixed at one guinea, with an entrance fee of one guinea. It was decided that in the International Match with Ireland on the 9th April at Dublin the selection of players be left to the same committee that selected the players for the English match. A vote of thanks to the chairman brought the meeting to a close.

The announcement of the foundation of the Welsh Rugby Union

the chair was the Swansea Captain, Mr C. C. Chambers (who had made complaints about the selection of both soccer and rugby teams), and the clubs now represented were Bangor, Brecon, Cardiff, Lampeter, Llandeilo, Llandovery, Llanelli, Merthyr, Newport, Pontypool and Swansea. For the next eleven years Mullock remained Secretary and one suspects that his standing remained unaltered despite the outcry. When one thinks that the referee of that first match, Arthur Guillemard, then the President of the Rugby Union, spoke freely of 'the unwashed portion of the British public' and noted that 'the ladies of Blackheath' alone contrived to keep off the touchline and so keep the field of play clear, it is probable that Mullock retained his office because he was the man for dealing with such men.

Wales has always had two kinds of heroes, those who succeed in England and those who, often extending themselves in a different direction, triumph closer to the ground at home. About the first, there is ever suspicion and one suspects Mullock was determined that Welsh football was going to be seen to be on a parity with our neighbours. Rowland Hill, later the Honorary Secretary of the Rugby Union, for a long period keeper of private records at Somerset House and for thirty

Rowland Hill, Secretary of the Rugby Union, who adjudicated tactfully over early complaints of Welsh professionalism.

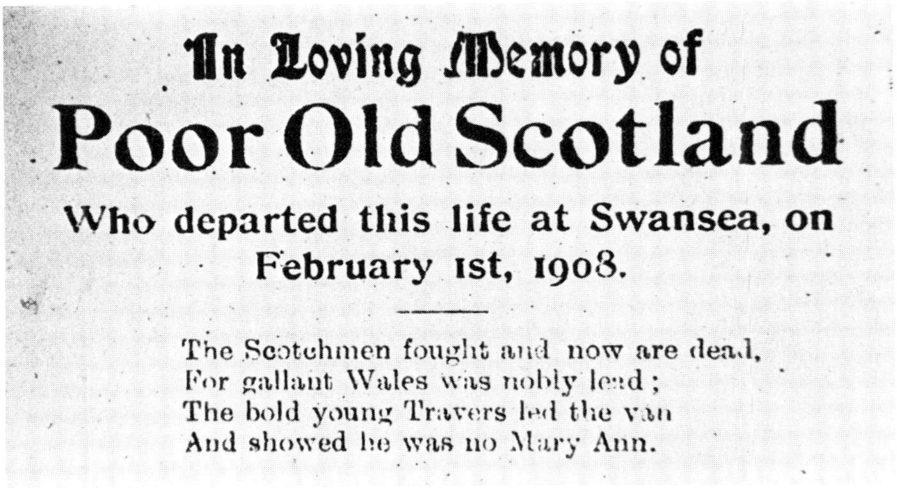
In Loving Memory of
Poor Old Scotland
Who departed this life at Swansea, on
February 1st, 1908.

The Scotchmen fought and now are dead,
For gallant Wales was nobly lead;
The bold young Travers led the van
And showed he was no Mary Ann.

Mourning cards handed to losers by jubilant supporters

years Chairman of Greenwich Conservative Association—'the Tory of Tories and the Amateur of Amateurs'—spoke of Mullock as 'a man of energy and perseverance', and when England 'consented to play Wales' (and by doing so set a good example to other nationalities!), he attributed 'the wonderful strides made' to Richard Mullock. Of his own Rugby Union, Rowland Hill wrote, 'no miserable personal animosities have ever crept in to spoil the harmony of their work', and one can imagine Mullock casting an envious eye over the border. As a printer, he might have been responsible for the joke mourning cards which cocky fans presented to each other, but little is known about him

In Loving Memory of
THE
South Africans
WHO WERE BEATEN BY
GOOD OLD CARDIFF,
New Year's Day, 1907.

'Twas a glorious victory, proclaim it all around,
How the mighty Springboks were vanquished on the famous
Cardiff Ground,
Though the Africans struggled hard to win, to everyone 'twas plain
That they had met their Masters, and lie numbered with the slain.

LOST, BUT NOT FORGOTTEN.

other than that he was a water colourist, and he seems to have faded into obscurity after relinquishing his connection with rugby football. The burly confident face which stares from team photographs of the period tells us very little and it is probable that he emigrated to Rhodesia having fallen upon hard times. There is a brief report in the *South Wales Daily News* of January 1902, which reveals that he found it difficult to support a wife and six children, stating that he earned a living 'drawing in black and white, having left off travelling'. It is thought that he paid out a good deal from his own pocket to contribute to the foundation of the Welsh Rugby Union and his original insistence on picking players who had learned their rugby at school or college was no more than a reflection of the practices which brought the game to Wales.

A. J. Gould

Evan James at work (kneeling centre) with copper-ladlers at White Rock Works, Swansea

The future would be very different for, in the words of that first referee, there were waiting 'a large proportion of tyros, very keen and full of pluck'. Among them were the catalysts of everything that followed, archetypal figures who would cast the die, like Evan and David James, the Swansea copper-ladlers who were to delight and enrage at half-back for Swansea and Wales, then to vanish. There was also Arthur Gould of Newport, the prince of three-quarters, whose royalty was never disputed and about whom controversy lingered like smoke. The James Brothers, it so happens, were half-Jewish and Gould's father hailed from Oxfordshire. Between them they were to grace the Prince of Wales' feathers as no one had done before, and Gould, in appearance the Omar Sharif of his day, was to rival any film star in the adulation which surrounded him. These men and others in every club were the heroes of a new age, and although they were not at first catapulted on to the world's stage as were the boxers of a later generation, they succeeded in the face of the disapproval of those religious bodies who saw the game as 'the fascination of the devil and the twin sister of the drinking system', a game which they thought encouraged drunkenness and violence and removed its participants from beyond their control. But while the deacons of Ystradgynlais went out and cut down the goal posts (which they did in 1890) and young men were encouraged to burn their jerseys and sign the pledge (as they were in Ynysybwl when the Revivalist preacher Evan Roberts spoke to such effect that he closed the rugby club down for three years) and the resentments towards this new society continued, the people had found their national game. It was already an expression of national identity and it was to stay, gathering its strength from the clubs.

Arthur 'Monkey' Gould, the prince of Welsh three-quarters, the first of the national idols, in appearance the Omar Sharif of Welsh rugby.

2

The First Greats

Five rugby clubs have dominated Welsh Rugby football at various times in the hundred years of the Welsh Rugby Union and with each of them famous players and distinctive eras are associated: Swansea, Cardiff, Newport, Llanelli and the London Welsh. Typically, the Welsh-based clubs often began their fixtures with the schools who brought the game to Wales: Swansea's first recorded game was against Llandovery College. This was in 1874 and it is probable that the recruitment of players differed in no way from Newport who first formed an association club in the same year. Finding it impossible to arrange fixtures under the association code, Newport played a rugby match at the end of the season with the Cardiff-based Glamorgan Rugby Club, arriving two men short and borrowing a Swansea man to make up thirteen. Some of the occupations of the players are known, with solicitors again to the fore, and there is every reason to suppose that the composition of these early teams was exactly as it was elsewhere. Fourteen years later, however, two brothers, Evan and David James, who worked in the White Rock copper works at Swansea, made their appearance in the Swansea side. They played first for the St Thomas Harlequins, then progressed to the Swansea team who even then ran a second fifteen, according to Arthur Gould who was to write about them. Their father had been a miner who had journeyed to Truro in Cornwall, worked in the tin mines, married a Jewess and then returned to Swansea where they set up house. His wife had been disinherited for marrying a Gentile, according to family legend, and the four children soon born to the couple were rather specially treated.

The James family, like another Swansea family soon to produce their own rugby giants, the Bancrofts, initially lived close to the Swansea ground, and it is highly likely that the James' most famous sons were witnesses as well as participants of the growing popularity of the game and the club. Mrs James, who later called Evan and David 'my Greek Gods' could probably do very little about the hubbub of rugby activity that went on within half a mile of the house. Although the brothers were destined to work in the copper works like their father, and later moved further away from the centre of Swansea, they must have had, like Swansea children ever since, an ever-present awareness of the *right*, The James brothers, Evan and David, who were nicknamed the 'Curly-Haired Marmosets' or the 'Pocket Halves'. Their Jewish mother called them 'My Greek Gods'. *below*, Swansea had a supporters' club called the Bowery Boys, of which two members are seen here in Caswell Bay in 1897. Only the curly brim of the bowler puts a date on the altogether!

rugby enthusiasms generated in the town. When the James brothers were boys, the Swansea club forged links with the ten amateur northern clubs like Salford and Wakefield Trinity, and it was commonplace for large numbers of Swansea followers to accompany the team on an away game. By 1888, there was even a Swansea Supporters' Club calling themselves the Bowery Boys who, following an away win at Cardiff, made a triumphant march through the town to the station. It was quite usual for the results of matches to be wired home and handbills printed to broadcast good news, and once the Swansea skipper was carried from the station down the High Street, followed by 'an immense concourse of persons'.

The other side of the Welsh coin were workmen and works' sides like the Chainworks Crusaders of Pontypridd. 'The private school game found its way to the public parks.'

ONTYPRIDD CHAINWORKS CRUSADERS FOOTBALL CLUB

'inners of "Glamorgan Times" Challenge Cup and Gold Medals, Season 1895-96

W. Whitehead J. Walsh J. Lifield T. Allen (Treasurer) T. Thomas (Vice-President) J. Casey W. Mackden W. Angurn
arry (Touch Judge) Tom Phillips (Secretary)
T. Morris I. Caple W. Wilkins (Captain) Ll. Whitehead (Vice-Captain) J. R. Jones A. Jones
J. Coslett I. Wilkins E. Morgan D. Morgan

The Western Stars Thursday Team, Aberavon, 1888. 'These early teams had a social cachet, their players a readiness to mix.'

Looking back, it is not difficult to imagine that the James brothers were caught up in this enthusiasm, and when the time came for them to take their own places in the team, they did so with startling results. It was not long before journalists found some graphic descriptions for them, 'The Pocket Halves', or 'The Curly-Haired Marmosets'. From the beginning they were always spoken of as a pair. They were different from other players in that their tricks with the ball and their bodies reminded onlookers 'more of circus performers than football contestants'. They would do handstands and cartwheels as they ran on to the field, and wherever they played they increased the size of crowds as their reputations spread. When they were first capped for Wales against Ireland at Llanelli, there was chaos on the railways. Said one captain who played against them, 'Go for the varmint who looks as if he hasn't got the ball because he's sure to have it!'

Evan and David James were described as the great innovators of half-back tactics and, in W. J. Townsend Collins' words, 'individual geniuses *and* geniuses in combination . . . Their handling was swift and sure, they dodged in little space, they feinted, they passed and re-passed and that so quickly that the opponents were bewildered.' Collins, the most reliable critic of the period, also made the reservation that: 'They were not completely effective links with the three-quarters for they were not so much concerned with what they enabled the team to do as with what they could do themselves.' But Arthur Gould who played against them was of the opinion that a great deal of their artifice came to

THE BROTHERS JAMES, SWANSEA.

nothing, 'through the inability of three-quarters to take advantage of the openings made for them'. He also believed that in the Welsh team at least, they were thrown upon their own resources to such an extent that their attacking power was more developed than it would have been had they been able to depend upon their backs! It was not that they were merely attacking players for Gould also states, 'They were deadly tacklers and fine defensive players. Never have I seen men more utterly fearless of danger on the football field, and the way they have stopped the rushes of enormous forwards has been simply marvellous. As for their pluck, one has only to remember that Evan James sustained serious injury to his shoulder soon after the English game began and yet played to the end. His brother is just as plucky.'

It seemed that they would sometimes take it in turns to put the ball into the scrum and often exchanged positions at half-back, so that they were forever associated with guile and were the most watched and marked members of any side in which they played. Legends grew up about their prowess and they were said to practise together, juggling with everything that bore any resemblance to a ball—loaves of bread, jugs, even the undertaker's top hat on one occasion. Mischief seems to have been a part of their game. Their fame spread when they suddenly disappeared from the Welsh rugby scene and went secretly to play for Broughton Rangers in Manchester, having originally been named to play against Barnstaple that same week. The Swansea Club alleged that the brothers made a demand on them for thirty shillings a match and, because the demand was not complied with, they left without regard to the ordinary rules of transference. At this time Yorkshire was advertising for players, offering first-class train fare, cigars, liquor and accommodation in four-star hotels. Early on there was the glint of foreign gold—and with it repercussions.

In Swansea the sense of loss was profound. 'Oh, where, oh where are the famous half-backs?' asked the rugby critic of the *Cambrian* on 27 January 1893. The question of professionalism in Welsh rugby football, which was to last until the present day, was raised in the most dramatic terms even providing the description of the gold-laden seducer from out of town, as a *Cambrian* journalist indicates:

To-night a committee will sit in solemn conclave to receive evidence relative to the flight of the brothers James from Swansea to Manchester when it is expected some startling statements will be made. The cast of the erstwhile Swansea halves is exciting great interest throughout the whole football world, for upon its result will depend the future of professionalism. For the brothers to deny they were induced to leave the home of their birth by pecuniary considerations is absurd on the face of it. No men would leave a town where they could get fairly regular work and pay and fly to a far distant town in the 'hope' of finding employment. Lancashire and Yorkshire people may believe such a 'cock and bull' story, but we in South Wales and those who conduct the Rugby affairs of England and Wales are not to be misled by such a story. My readers would probably like to know the circumstances under which the 'curly-headed marmosets' left Swansea.

A few days prior to their sudden flight, a Swansea man was in High Street, when he was accosted by a well-dressed man who appeared to be a stranger to the town.

'Could you tell me where I could see the brothers James, the famous half-backs?' he said.

The Swansea man gazed somewhat at his questioner and with a merry and wicked twinkle in his eyes, replied: 'Yes, I know where they are, but what do you want them for?'

'Oh, I am a cousin of theirs and have not seen them for some years. I belong to Gloucester and have just run down for a trip.'

The twinkle in the Swansea man's eye grew merrier and more wicked. 'Get along with you,' he said. 'Do you think I don't know a Gloucester man from a Lancashire man, I know what you want. You want them to play for some club.'

The stranger seemed taken by surprise . . . 'Well, eh, as you have pressed my object I think I may as well tell you that a club in Manchester is hard up for a pair of half-backs. We want a good pair. Do you think we could get the brothers James? Are they hard to satisfy?'

* * *

The stranger had in mind princely jobs as warehousemen which 'could be made worth £2 a week', and a few days later the James brothers played for 'a club near Manchester'. The attention given to the matter in local newspapers was so great that the correspondence columns even contained protests at the amount of newspaper attention given to 'common labourers', and there were allegations that they had forsaken the town which petted and fêted them at the first opportunity, even though 'money was placed in their clothes by some of their well-to-do admirers'.

Their departure meant the loss of a star pair of entertainers and locally there was a feeling of being let down. They had practised their tricks and subtleties to the bewilderment of all their foes and were now to help Broughton Rangers win the Lancashire Cup. There you might think the matter would have ended as did similar journeys made by many famous players later. But after three years the critical views of those who had been disappointed were to alter when it was known that the James brothers wished to return and the Rugby Union offered some objection because of the violation of the transfer laws. This was before the split between the northern clubs and, when the question of their reinstatement as Swansea players was discussed, there were accusations that the English Rugby Union were treating Welsh football 'as if it did not exist'. For the first time a question of national pride was raised. The laws were obviously not as stringent as they were to become and, as a result of pressure by the Swansea Club, the Welsh Rugby Union met at Cardiff to discuss their appeal. It is said that one of the reasons for the James brothers wanting to return was home-sickness, and the interest aroused in Swansea was such that on the night of the official meeting when the Welsh Rugby Union undoubtedly had contact with Rowland Hill, a searchlight was held in readiness on the roof of a local ironmonger's and arrangements were made to signal the news. A rotating flash was to indicate reinstatement, and a straight steady light the reverse. It is said that the town 'rocked with joy' when it was learned that they had been reinstated. A torchlight procession took place and the Swansea club (who had already picked their team with the half-back places left blank!) were impresarios once more. On the following Saturday, the James brothers ran out on to the field to opposing ends of the touchline in order to 'salute and bow their acknowledgements'.

The letter of reinstatement from Rowland Hill is curt and to the point. It is probable that he bowed to Welsh pressure and it is not difficult to imagine his feelings when, in January 1899, the James

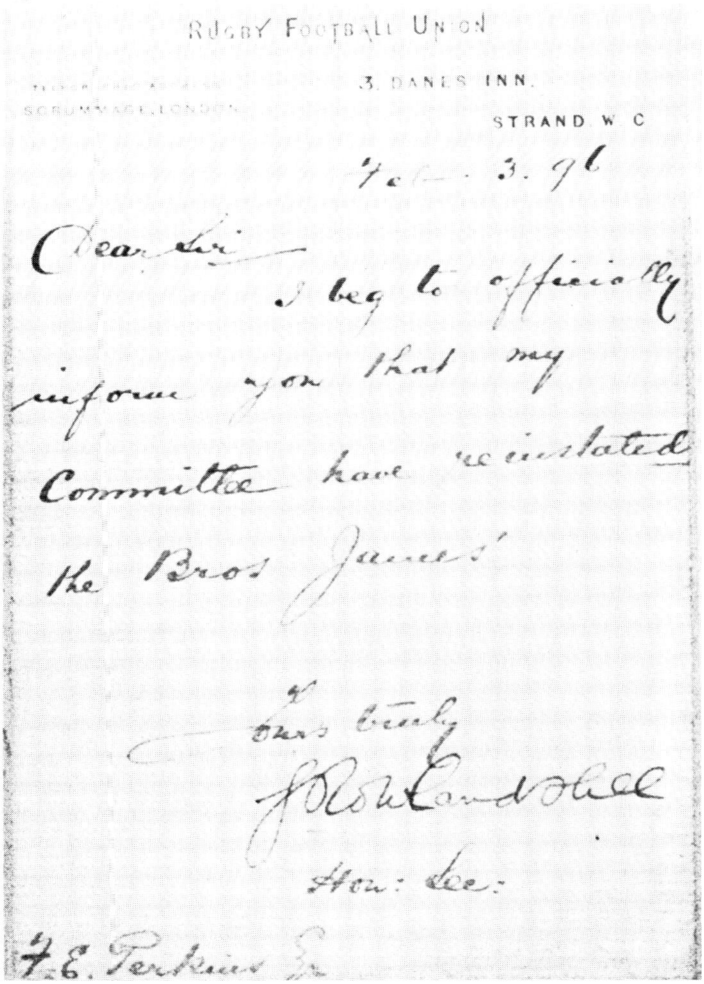

RUGBY FOOTBALL UNION

SCRUMMAGE, LONDON

3, DANES INN,

STRAND W C

Feb. 3. 96

Dear Sir

I beg to officially inform you that my Committee have reinstated the Bros James

Yours truly

G Rowland Hill

Hon: Sec:

F. E. Perkins Esq

The letter sent to Swansea RFC from Rowland Hill, Secretary of the RFU, reinstating the Swansea half-backs brothers were selected to play for Wales once more at Swansea and he saw England lose by twenty-six points to three. Even though Evan, just over five foot six and under ten stone, broke his collar-bone in the first five minutes, the rout was completed before a record crowd which was twice the size of that of the previous year, one reporter stating, 'The English captain, Rotherham, wasted a good deal of energy in empty protests when he found the brothers James too good for him.'

Another famous Welsh three-quarter, Willie Llewellyn, made a spectacular début that day, scoring four tries on the left wing, and the adulatory fever he generated on that occasion was to continue all his life and indeed long after he had retired. His chemist's shop, which was situated in the main street of Tonypandy, was one of the few left unmolested during bitter industrial riots.

No sooner had the James brothers reestablished themselves and drawn praise from all corners, however, than they were off again. They vanished from Swansea twelve days after the English match with their whole family, sixteen in all including grandmother, with tickets for Manchester and new playing contracts for the brothers. They now received £200 each in sovereigns and £2 a match, and both were provided with houses. But the north was never to claim them wholly. From the start, David's wife was laughed at for carrying a baby Welsh-fashion in a shawl on Manchester station, and she could not abide the back-to-back houses or the noise of clogs on the cobbles. She was Welsh-speaking, from the Swansea valley village of Bonymaen, and after a season the family returned to make their home in her village. Evan died of tuberculosis at the age of thirty while David declined the offer of a job as rugby coach at Mill Hill School and returned to the copperworks where he resumed work as a copper-ladler. He was described as a shy man with a pronounced stammer and marked sense of humour. Mischief seems to have been a part of his life for he named his eldest son Jesse after the western desperado and was only just prevented from calling his second son Frank by his more patriotic wife who preferred Llewellyn. At his funeral his rugby caps were laid along the organ and to this day his house is reported haunted by a mischievous ghost who throws things.

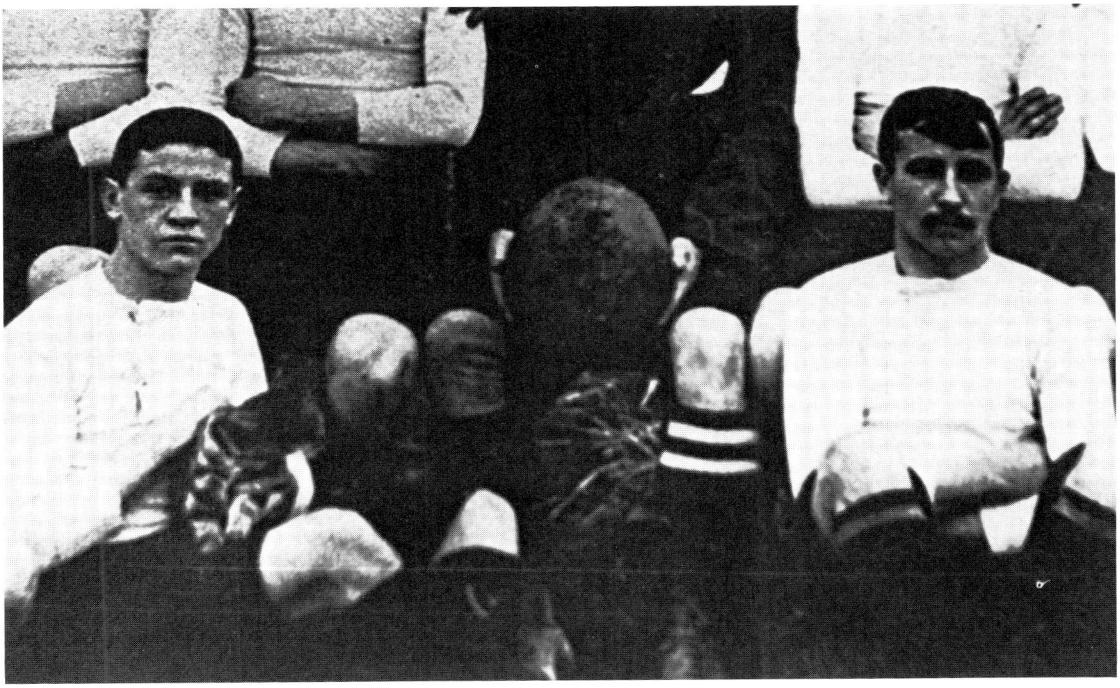

The 'Curly-Haired Marmosets' were followed by 'The Dancing Dicks', Richard Owen (left) and Richard Jones (right)

For all the legend that surrounds the James brothers, their lifestyle was not materially affected by the rewards of rugby football for any length of time and David, like a number of famous players of his era, positively dissuaded his children from playing the game at its most competitive level. The influence of the James brothers remained, nevertheless, and very soon the Swansea club had another pair of international half-backs, Richard Owen and Richard Jones, known appropriately as the Dancing Dicks, who were to be even more successful for Wales and Swansea. A significant tradition had begun, and while it was said that there was a time when the half-back break was considered bad form, like potting your opponent's white at billiards, there is no doubt that the Welsh half-backs of those years, as their nicknames imply, were the ingenious and inventive darlings of the crowd. They offered wit and inventiveness, developing a style of play which was handed down and improved upon, always showing a flair

Two faces of Dicky Owen, nicknamed 'The Bullet', the scrum-half of the first Golden Era

which led to the increase in popularity of the game. They also, of course, increased gate money which was becoming important both in England and Wales. There is a story concerning Blackheath who came to play Swansea in 1891 and were offered half the proceeds of the gate money but rejected the offer, insisting on a small fixed sum which could be guaranteed. When they arrived to see a large crowd of fifteen thousand they attempted to revert to the original offer but were refused, with the result that fixtures were cancelled for nearly fifty years.

Half-backs like the James brothers were not the only attraction, nor were the games—whether club matches or internationals—free of the incidents which have come to characterise rugby football at its most competitive. When the James brothers played against Scotland at Swansea in 1892, ten players were injured, David James was badly cut, a Scot was taken to hospital, and 'a mob of cowardly blackguards swept down and set about the referee' who was only saved when Arthur Gould and others bundled him into a cab and accompanied him to the safe refuge of the Mackworth Hotel. Scotland won on this occasion, as they did a year earlier when an indifferent Welsh performance in Edinburgh was attributed by one apologist to the upset the Welsh team received by being taken, a few hours before the game, 'to the dissecting rooms of Edinburgh University Hospital'.

Reason, then as now, could go out of the window when passions were aroused. One player, the same man who had been knocked down by a punch intended for the referee on that dismal afternoon at St Helens, Swansea, became the most praised, the most controversial, and probably the best known rugby player of his decade, Arthur Gould of Newport. It is Gould, in fact, who might be taken as the very symbol of that new sense of identity, for it was he who aroused the most heat when the question of his amateur status was raised at the end of his career. As a result of a testimonial fund raised to reward him at the end of his international career in 1897, both Scotland and Ireland refused to play Wales, and England prohibited the clubs from playing against him. Yet this was the man who wrote: 'We seem to be drifting towards a stage where money or "pots", the material rewards or symbols of

LONDON: SATURDAY NIGHT, FEBRUARY 27, 1897.

A BACKYARD QUARREL.

MRS. ENGLAND. You shan't come and play in our yard: I don't like you any more.

MISS WALES. You'll be sorry when you see me Swinging on our garden door.

MRS. SCOTLAND & MRS. IRELAND. You shan't holler down our rain-barrel, You shan't climb our apple-tree.

MISS WALES. I don't want to play in your yard, If you won't be good to me.

success, are valued highly, striven for strenuously and manoeuvred for trickily while the honour of victory, the joy of contest, the glory of achievement are no longer the stimulating and sustaining principle of the athletes. There is much of the same spirit in many walks of life and it is not good for the nation that it should be so.'

The conundrum is not easily explained unless we consider that

Gould, unlike the James brothers, was altogether more sophisticated and came to the game from a background that was probably much more like that of his counterparts playing for English clubs, although it was his club of Newport which taught him the game, not a public school. His attitudes were undoubtedly anglicised, but it was his person which was caught up in the immense veneration for the game. The son of a prosperous Newport brass founder, he was one of five rugby-playing brothers, three of whom were capped for Wales, and he was also a track sprinter and a hurdler who was several times placed in the English Championships. In his lifetime he also played for English clubs in Hampshire and Middlesex, and it was evident from his very first game for Newport at the age of sixteen as an emergency full-back that he was one of those different players who seem to have all the gifts. 'Kick, you little devil!' the Newport captain is reported to have shouted in that first match, but Gould twice ran through the opposition to score tries.

W. J. Townsend Collins wrote of Gould:

> As a footballer, he had all the gifts and they had been developed by thought and constant practice. Some boys when they begin to play rugby football find that they dodge, swerve and sidestep naturally—it is not a question of thought, it is an animal instinct. Arthur Gould was one of them. He dodged and swerved away from a tackler instinctively, but before he had gone far he had learned to study the capacity of his fellow players and the defensive powers of his opponents, knew what he was doing, why he did it and how it was done. Other players on their inspired days had gone through their opponents—swerving, sidestepping, dodging with easy mastery which made the defence look silly; other centres have made perfect openings and unselfishly given their wings chances to score; other men have nipped their opponents' attacks in the bud by the quickness with which they smothered man and ball, or by intercepting passes; others have tackled man after man or compelled them to pass after being taken with the ball; but no three-quarter I have known has maintained the high level of attainment in attack and defence so long and so consistently as Arthur Gould. No man has shown such

> uniform brilliance and resourcefulness over so long a period of years.

Few rugby players can have had such an epitaph and Gould was to win twenty-seven caps between 1885 and 1897. He certainly owed something to the most historic of all the Welsh contributions to the game, the introduction of the four three-quarter system which was actually begun by an English brewer, Frank Hancock, who came to Cardiff to live and play. At first Gould was against it, but he was captain in 1893 when Wales with four three-quarters won their first triple crown, defeating the other three nations. Gould was carried from the Arms Park at Cardiff to the nearby Angel Hotel, sending, in the words of a correspondent, 'the population half off their chumps'.

Gould said later, after a convincing win against Scotland, that 'the moral effect of our victory will be to compel the Scots and the English clubs to play the Welsh style.' He was probably talking about method rather than style, but there is no question that a style was formed, and the Reverend Marshall's early history of the game attributed the special characteristics of the Welsh style of play to the concentration of the Welsh clubs in a small geographical area where they continually played amongst themselves. Then as now it is probable that players like Gould brought their skill to perfection as a result of this fierce competitiveness, but whereas today we are too often locked in struggles of forward supremacy, players of Gould's calibre were able to put their stamp upon the game in the same way as did Bleddyn Williams and Lewis Jones. These men both had that speed of thought and foot and the ability to beat men as if by mesmerising them which has become rare amongst mid-field players. This Welsh style was born, according to Marshall, 'because the Welshmen had to make up for the paucity of their numbers by science in play', and when they were beaten, they were defeated 'by superior weight, strength and speed' which had broken down 'the system carefully planned by the wily ingenious Taffs'. Marshall wrote this in 1892 and for years there were protests at Welsh rehearsals of tactics, of sides 'planning', so much so that one suspects the international board ruling which prevented players from training together on more

Lewis Jones (Llanelli, Wales and the British Lions) who epitomised Welsh flair, the ability to do the unexpected with style and grace, his speed of thought and foot unique. He created tries from the full-back position which caused him to be described as the best full-back to have visited New Zealand since the war.

than one occasion before an international match was specifically enforced just because of the Welsh. It was a ruling that lasted for nearly three decades and Bleddyn Williams, writing shortly after his own playing career ended, comments, 'It does not seem fair that a player representing his country for the first time should be expected to combine with and understand the various unorthodox movements of his fellow players after approximately one hour on the practice field! Some followers of the game advocate that a player of international class should fit into any combination, but I cannot agree with this line of thought and it is my contention that confidence plays a tremendous part in the failure or success of an international player.'

Arthur Gould wearing his legendary martyr's crown

Nearly seventy years earlier, Gould had written: 'If our Welsh team could practise together it would be different, then you could have your best men and they would learn each other's play. But inferior men thoroughly in touch with each other will often give a far better and more effective exposition of our game than cracks chosen from different clubs who will require some little shaking together ere they can easily accommodate their play.'

The international board ruling preventing practice lasted until the present decade and, while it was often palliated by the fact that numbers of players from the same clubs would, or course, have practised together, it has often meant that Welsh international sides have not been as effective as Welsh clubs. But confidence is another matter, and what Arthur Gould gave to the game was a princely confidence which seems to have shone through everything he did and wrote. Like players of today, he wrote about the game soon after he finished playing and he also served as a Welsh selector. His playing record apart, he seems to have been the kind of man who attracted gifts as well as praise, and it is extraordinary in this time of partisan loyalties to record that when he interrupted his career to take a job in the West Indies as a surveyor, a farewell dinner in Newport was attended by the representatives of many Welsh clubs who came bearing gifts and good wishes as if a tribal chief were departing. Indeed, much later in his life when he refereed a match in Plymouth, local worthies gave a reception for him, issuing tickets stating the privilege—'To meet A. J. Gould'.

He was thus one of the first rugby players to become a celebrity in the modern sense and he was catapulted off the sports pages by his decision to retire from international football, indicating his wish not to make himself available for the Welsh team after the match against Ireland in 1893. He had suffered recurrently from what was probably cartilage trouble, and in an interview with a correspondent of the *London Star* he

'Newport will miss him, Arthur has passed away.' (*Daily Mail*)

gave his views on the game, ironically pointing a finger at the very thing of which he was to be accused himself, stating that in his view the Association code was being ruined for amateur players by professionalism. 'Money v. money excites little of that local patriotism which obtains among our boys who grow up and revel in the game for its own sake.' He was, he said, 'strongly against professionalism of any kind'. There was an immediate response in the Press when he was described as the player of the century and 'The Passing of Arthur' was duly recorded with a sense of irreparable loss and obituaries to his playing career, although he had expressed his intention of continuing to play for Newport if required. The warmth and good feeling of his admirers can be imagined and a Cardiff journalist writing under the pseudonym 'Old Stager' was doing no more than expressing a popular view when he concluded a report in the *South Wales Daily News* with a seemingly innocuous suggestion:

> He is thus to the rugby game what W. G. Grace is to the sister pastime. What do Welsh footballers say to the proposition that the veteran's inestimable services to the game, which is still growing in popularity in Wales, should be recognised in the form of the presentation to him of a national testimonial?

Within an hour the Cardiff Coal Exchange, then the temple of a booming coal trade, had begun a shilling testimonial fund and soon sent a cheque for £50 to the editor as the first contribution. It was obviously a suggestion that met with universal approval. The matter snowballed and the Welsh Rugby Union were so far in accord with the idea that they themselves voted £50 towards the fund but, before this could be handed over, the Rugby Union in London entered a protest against its payment. The Welsh Union, not wishing to compromise Gould, finally withdrew its contribution, immediately heaping criticism upon itself. First came the shock of Gould's retirement, probably widely felt with the sense of loss that attends the retirements of great players of our own day, then the feeling of a need to commemorate the occasion, and at a half-way stage, the Welsh Rugby Union's caution which was seen to be an act of obeisance to London, always an emotive subject. 'The desire of our Union to be thought ultra pure is positively sickening,' wrote a correspondent, and comparisons were again made with Dr W. G. Grace who had received a handsome testimonial on his retirement. But that was cricket.

Gould himself said: 'If I were a young player who showed promise and the testimonial had been raised in order to prevent me from leaving Newport to go somewhere else, there might be some suggestion of professionalism, but here am I at the end of my career and there was no suggestion of that sort about the testimonial.' It is clear that he understood what was probably going on in the game, that is, that inducements were being offered to players to change clubs, but that he excluded himself from this tarnish, and he indicated his hostility to the

Rugby Union. 'I suppose they will want me to say that I must not watch a game of football; but I won't have a testimonial on those terms.'

It seems probable that the Welsh Rugby Union's tact was misinterpreted, but it led unwittingly to an increase in the public contributions and Gould's popularity increased as did the resentment of what was seen to be interference. Later, as the fund multiplied, the Welsh Union disputed the authority of the Rugby Union to interfere, stating that no universally agreed rules had been set out, but the argument continued with the result that the international match with Scotland was cancelled. There now followed an even greater argument and the press cartoonists began to enjoy themselves, for very soon it was planned to buy Gould a house with the money raised. Ireland had also

WELSH FOOTBALL INDEPENDENCE.

FIRM STAND BY THE WELSH RUGBY UNION.

STRAIGHT REPLY TO THE INTERNATIONAL BOARD.

DECLINES TO ACCEPT THE GOULD RESOLUTIONS.

SCOTTISH MATCH CANCELLED.

IMPORTANT DEVELOPMENTS EXPECTED.

PROBABLE FORMATION OF A NEW UNION.

WEST AND SOUTH OF ENGLAND WITH WALES.

NOTICE TO RESCIND THE NEW RULES.

UNPRECEDENTED EXCITEMENT IN FOOTBALL CIRCLES.

Gould was eventually presented with a house and a new set of laws was adopted

refused to play Wales and England prohibited its clubs from playing against any side that contained Gould, although not without protest from some of the English clubs, like Rockcliffe, who did not want to lose the Welsh connection. Dr Grace himself, an interested spectator of a rugby match between Pontypridd Police and the Bristol City Police was tact personified when questioned on the matter, stating that he thought it a pity the testimonial had not been discussed after the rugby season was over! But the dispute continued, the Welsh Rugby Union insisting on its right to adjudicate in its own affairs, and when the testimonial (which had by this time topped £500) was presented to Gould, it was in the form of the deeds of a house at Clytha Park, Newport, and the presenter was Sir John Llewellyn, President of the Welsh Rugby Union. There was a banquet at the Drill Hall in

above, The International Muddle
Wales to England, Scotland, and Ireland: 'Will you play us again?' Chorus: 'Yes, if you leave that bad boy Gould out.'

left, Wales: 'Let us give Prince Arthur a house.' International Board (decorated with cap and bells): 'If you give him a house or money you will be professionals, and if you keep them you are professionals.'
Wales: 'This is our affair, and we shall do as we please.'

Newport on Easter Monday, April 1897, and it seems to have been very much a tribal feast of victory. Ladies were in attendance in the gallery and Gould himself, the most capped player of his day, sat among civic and sporting worthies, including D. A. Thomas the coal owner (later Lord Rhondda). Thomas proposed the toast of the Newport Club with a few wisecracks about those in Wales who had disapproved of the advance of the rugby game and identified Gould very much as a symbol of modern Wales. Among those present was the captain of the English team and the players of Rockcliffe who had played a match against Newport that day. Gould had also played and dropped a goal, the restrictions having been ignored. It was a gala occasion with 250 guests and when the scarlet-clad band of the South Wales Borderers played *See the Conquering Hero Come* Gould got to his feet and waited modestly for the applause to die down. Although there had been a dispute, he felt it necessary to say that all the members of the international board were personal friends of his, and that what they had done they had done honestly in the best interests of the game. What he personally had done for Welsh football, he added, he had done from the heart. You can imagine the response, and it is unlikely that he ever made an enemy after that.

Gould got his house, his admirers got their way, and an upsurge of national feeling had crystallised a determination on the part of the representatives of the Welsh clubs not to be dictated to by others. The resolution of the position of stalemate was provided by the tact of Rowland Hill who, despite strong opposition, 'recognised the exceptional circumstances of the case'. A subsequent meeting between the two Unions produced agreement and a new set of professional laws was adopted, 'with the purpose of bringing the Welsh professional laws in line with those of England'. Wales had to make a plainer statement about the amateur code and it is perhaps true that Rowland Hill's tact (and the pressure of those English clubs who did not want a recurrence of the northern split) was the only answer to the suspicions and animosities that were felt elsewhere. In the words of a contemporary observer, 'If Wales declines (*to make a plainer statement about the amateur code*), she will show her real sentiments unveiled and naked in their true

THE TESTIMONIAL PRESENTED.

A. J. G. in Enjoyment of Repose.

RESTING UPON HIS LAURELS
AND ENJOYING THE *ARGUS* FOOTBALL EDITION

meaning, and not concealed under the guise of national admiration for an exceptional player.'

No doubt the English Union had had enough troubles in the north to contend with and the gift was the last of its kind, although admirers from five continents subscribed £1000 to endow the Arthur Gould Memorial Bed in the Royal Gwent Hospital in Newport. Gould, nicknamed 'Monkey' because of his youthful ability to climb trees, represents more than any other man the skill and confidence which the great players of the era brought to the game. Like the James brothers he was something special, and while there were many others who were free of controversy and played a Saturday game which they loved, Gould's achievements can be seen as the pinnacle of those early years. He was a clubman. He had been taught the game by the club and owed nothing to his schoolmasters, unlike so many of the players of the next era. The process of movement from private school to public park had completed an arc and the return movement was still to come, although the game in Wales, as Gould himself observed, was already regarded more from the point of view of the public than the players, an aspect which was to be demonstrated with the arrival of the first New Zealand touring side in 1905.

By then twenty-four years had passed since the first international match between Wales and England at the Rectory Field in Blackheath in 1881, and the words of R. H. B. Summers, one of the Welsh three-quarters that day, were already describing another decade:

> We changed at a small old-fashioned inn nearby. When we got to our changing room, we discovered that we were two men short, their invitations apparently having gone astray. However, we picked up two 'Varsity men with Welsh qualifications, and they agreed to fill the vacancies on condition that they were allowed to play three-quarter. The game was played before a small crowd of rugby enthusiasts ranged perhaps three deep around the ground.
>
> Lennie Stokes, the English captain, had the most to do with our downfall. He had a most baffling swerving run, and his left foot

> kicking broke our forwards' hearts for we had never seen a player who was able to kick with his left foot before. The Blackheath crowd called Stokes the bloody snipe. But in spite of the odds, we never gave up trying and at the dinner that night we were much encouraged when Stokes said, 'I have seen enough to know that you Welshmen will be hard to beat in a few years' time when you get together.'

By 1905 we had got it together and it is not difficult to imagine how it looked to those who awaited the all-conquering New Zealand side which came to Cardiff Arms Park in December 1905. If you had lived

A souvenir medal from the Wales v. New Zealand match

The Welsh team, Wales v. New Zealand, 1905

in Swansea, your milk might very well have been delivered by Dickie Owen, the foremost of the Dancing Dicks, who was in the process of winning his thirty-five caps as scrum-half for Wales. At just under eight stone he was one of the smallest men ever to play for Wales, and his record of caps which stood until after the second war must represent a peak of physical endurance that can hardly have been surpassed. His scowling button of a face, often taut, strained and prematurely aged, stares from the team photographs like that of a miniature James Cagney. Stories abound about him. By repute a chain-smoker who was not averse to a puff behind the posts during a club game, there is something morose and intense about the face, and if he had backed up the steps carrying a milk crate, I fancy you would look twice even if you did not know him. Like all scrum-halves he depended upon his pack a good deal, and in some ways he must have been a product of the general improvement in Welsh forward play of his time.

George Travers, Wales' first specialised hooker, who died while listening to a radio commentary of a match between Wales and the New Zealand Army Touring Team in 1947

There was a breed known as the Rhondda Forward who need not necessarily be from the valleys, but was probably a bigger, brasher version of what journalists had earlier described as 'the bashing type of Yorkshire Forward'. They had to be ball-winners of necessity and in Wales, with backs like Gwyn Nicholls, Rhys Gabe, Percy Bush, Willie Llewellyn and Teddy Morgan, the aristocrats of Welsh three-quarter play of the period and the equal by repute of any back today, the forwards knew what they had to do. Among them, waiting for that classic encounter, was George Travers, a coal trimmer from the Pill District of Newport whose working life was spent on the docks and whose loyalty to a little dockyard club, Pill Harriers, was to last his lifetime. Most of the glamour of this decade of Welsh rugby, the first golden era, has gone to its half-backs and three-quarters, but Travers belies the idea of the piano-shifter and an open letter of admiration to him on his retirement gives some idea of the debt that men like Dickie Owen owed to him.

> The truth is, George, you are not a hooker in the ordinary sense, but a scientific scrummager. You have done more than any forward I

A commemorative medal for George Travers

know to disprove the idea that all a forward has to do is stick his head in the scrum and shove the hardest. Weight no doubt counts for much if properly utilised in the pack, but you have done much to educate the masses in the art of forward play, and at the same time shown them that something besides weight is essential in a forward. 'How does George Travers get the ball?' they ask. The single answer I can think of is brains.

George Travers won twenty-five caps for Wales and was founder of a rugby dynasty of rugby-playing sons, including Bill Travers who was to occupy his father's position in the Welsh team before and after the Second World War.

Bill Travers at work and play

The Travers family, artisans all. *left to right, standing*: Jim (Monmouthshire Police), Leonard (Newport), W. H. 'Bunner' (Newport, Wales, British Lions), George; *left to right, seated, wearing caps*: Jack (Newport), George (Pill Harriers, Newport and Wales), Matthew (Newport)

Perhaps more than any family they represent the solid core of the game, and the pack which Wales was to assemble in 1905 contained other men like them who were all drilled in the art of ball-winning, men like the collier and police constable, Dai 'Tarw' Jones from Treherbert who brought what was then a rare sixteen stone to bear. There was, with one or two exceptions, an occupational line drawn in the side. Most of the other forwards were manual workers and, unlike the very first Welsh team, nearly all of whom were at Oxford or Cambridge, there were no Oxbridge men. Percy Bush and Rhys Gabe had been to training college, Teddy Morgan was a doctor, Willie Llewellyn a chemist, and Gwyn Nicholls ran a laundry business with Winfield the full-back. Like them, Percy Bush, the fly-half, had been on tour with the British team in Australia and New Zealand the previous year.

The Welsh team of 1905 was knowledgeable, experienced and truly representative of the game in Wales in exactly the same way as was the New Zealand side. One can imagine that this side, which had not been beaten at home for six years, viewed the arrival of the New Zealanders with interest from the moment they played their first game in Devon where they defeated the county side by fifty-five points to four.

Reports were obviously closely studied in Wales and what caught the attention of observers was the New Zealand captain Dave Gallaher. He was first described as a winger on the edge of the scrum, in reality a wing-forward who did not pack down, thereby probably incurring some of the legacies of disapproval for the work-shy forwards of earlier

Dai 'Tarw' Jones, the hard man of the Welsh pack of 1905

years who, because they did not push their weight and were ever anxious to shine in the open, were described as going in for 'winging', a strong criticism which took no account of the fact that some packs like the New Zealanders might be able to manage with just seven forwards. Early Press comments were detailed.

'With regard to the visitors' style of play and arrangement on the field . . . here are seven forwards who form up lines of two, three, two. The winger (wing-forward) is nothing more nor less than a half-back whose business it is to prevent the opposing scrum worker from getting the ball away to the three-quarters. He never goes in the scrum, though he sometimes puts the ball in, and as the winger is the New Zealand captain and the tallest man in the team, a small half has no chance of doing anything.' And in the Devon match the little home scrum-half had been pulverised, one of many pieces information which Owen must have read with interest as the tour progressed.

There were other oddities. Gillet, the New Zealand full-back wore a cap and Gallaher strapped his shin guards outside his stockings, a habit which irritated some journalists. The Press began to devote more and more space to the tour after Cornwall were defeated. Then Bristol was defeated by a cricket score when the Welsh selectors were present, including Arthur Gould who no doubt reported back. The New Zealand seven-forward formation interested everyone and Gallaher was in no doubt about its superiority: 'I have been asked many questions as to my opinion of the merits of our packing as compared with English methods. Every man in my team has his allotted place, and on scrumming each man goes down in his own place. We do not waste time in this way, having put in a great deal of practice, and, as the result has been that with seven men we have held eight opponents, surely further comment is unnecessary.'

The New Zealanders were not averse to practice and had the advantage which every touring side has of playing regularly together. Their victories continued and Northampton, Leicester and Middlesex fell to an ever-increasing aggregate of points scored, with a miserable total in reply. And the comments continued: 'It was not so much what they did that nonplussed their opponents, but the quickness with which

A set scrum in New Zealand territory, Wallace on right, Gillett at back, to left of Wallace. Note referee in street clothes to left of scrum.

they did it. Not only was the passing clean and accurate, but the passers and takers were both going at full speed when they gave or took the ball. The result was that no half-and-half tackling had any chance of being successful.'

After the Hartlepools went down by sixty-three points to nil, the critics waxed eloquent. 'It was a refinement of rugby—rugby intellectualised; rugby metamorphosed.'

Soon there was a band-wagon effect and, with the tour results standing at 310 points to seven scored against, the New Zealand High Commissioner chipped in. He was not surprised that the British public was amazed at the brilliance of his footballers. 'The conditions which make for the development of a fine race of athletes are a plentiful supply of good food of all descriptions, the reasonably short hours worked by the men, allowing leisure for sport, exercise and recreation, and the careful guarding of the lives of the women and children by the operation of strict sanitary regulations. Families are somewhat smaller in

The New Zealand Fifteen singing their Maori War Cry prior to the opening of their first International match against Scotland at Inverleith, 1905

New Zealand than in England. This, no doubt, ensures a better and more healthy upbringing for the children, a fact which weighs considerably in the rearing of a strong healthy race.'

There could seldom have been a better opportunity for a public relations exercise and the tour manager added his own explanation. 'You see, it's a national affair with us, much as your cricket 'ashes' expedition was with you. Rugby Football is the New Zealand national game, every boy in the colony plays it, and this team, chosen by almost national assent, is the result of much care and thought. It represents the manhood and virility of the colony.'

If ever there was a case of cards on the table, this was it, and when Oxford and Cambridge were beaten and the rout continued, there was a good deal of self-examination in the English Press. The *Daily Mail* received a large number of explanations to the query, 'Why do the New Zealanders always win?'

'Because they are "brainy" players,' wrote a correspondent from Northampton, and added his own diagnosis. 'There is no caste in the New Zealanders' composition; they have sporting heads on their shoulders and are welded into one harmonious whole. Innovations are odious to the English people and to cavil and criticise the formation on the field of the New Zealand players is spiteful. . . .'

The inquest continued but Arthur Gould was not all that impressed and pointed out that the victories achieved could well have been equalled by the previous year's Welsh side. There must have been some relief when Scotland put up a hard fight and only lost by seven points to twelve on a frost-bound and slippery ground. The Scottish players went unrewarded however.

'No caps were given to the Scottish XV and this display of parsimony has been adversely commented upon on both sides of the border. It appears that when the fixture was arranged, the Scottish Rugby Union authorities, doubting the "drawing" properties of the New Zealanders, refused to give the required guarantee of £200 and, instead, decided to let them take the whole of the gate, minus expenses. As the receipts from the match amounted to over £1000, there was considerable soreness in official circles at missing such a grand opportunity of swelling union coffers. Hence, it was stated, the determination not to award caps to the Scottish XV.' The Scottish Rugby Union also insisted that the match ball kept by the All Blacks as a souvenir of the game be returned, and fixtures with the 1924 All Blacks were first refused because they believed that the three-shilling allowance per day professionalised them.

Ireland went down fifteen points to nil, and so did England by the same score, while Yorkshire, without its professional players, of course, lost by forty points and the professional players who were watching were not very impressed. 'The wearers of the silver fern have not been defeated, but they have not played the cream of English football.' (They had their eyes on one or two of the New Zealand players who were to return to play professionally, however!) The points tally by this time read twenty-seven games played and won, with 801 points for to twenty-two against. All the rugby world was looking to Cardiff.

The Welsh games had been left until the last and New Zealand were without three of their best players who were injured or unfit. They might or might not have noticed that, on the Saturday previous to the last international, the Welsh selectors (of whom Gould was one) had made a request to the Cardiff club who were playing Blackheath in London. They had asked that Willie Llewellyn of Llwynypia and Teddy Morgan of the London Welsh should replace regular Cardiff players and play outside Nicholls and Gabe, the regular Welsh centres, and that A. F. Harding, also of the London Welsh, should be transferred to Cardiff for the day. The displaced Cardiff players agreed to play for the London Welsh. Thus the entire Welsh three-quarter line, the fly-half and the full-back, had a run-out in the Cardiff jersey, and no doubt when Dickie Owen left his milk round on the Friday before the game, the move which was to result in the only try of the match was hatched.

From the start the New Zealanders knew that Percy Bush, the Welsh outside-half, was something special. They had already seen him in New Zealand and the idea of the Welsh fly-half in the classic mould was well established. At the centre of it was the ability to beat a man by sidestepping or dummying, accelerating or swerving and Bush was known for his elusive running. He would therefore be a marked man and this was something to be played upon.

It is not difficult to imagine the excitement building up. It was to be a case of Greek meeting Greek, for the game had become the national game of Wales, drawing its recruits from all sources in exactly the same way as it had done in New Zealand. At home the success of Welsh sides at club and international level increased expectations and militated against the idea of running out on the field and offering passive resistance—this had been done by so many English sides so that the Welsh must run at them. From the start, all the elements of a cauldron about to boil were present and there began on this occasion a long period of rivalry between Wales and New Zealand. The report of A. J. Buttery gives us some idea of the occasion.

All Blacks' First Defeat. Were They Spellbound?
by J. A. Buttery

The all-conquering 'All Blacks' at last tasted the bitterness of defeat. After twenty-seven consecutive victories—nearly all of them of the most electrifying character—over the pick of English, Irish, and Scottish rugby football sides, they were beaten by Wales, at Cardiff, by one try to nothing, amid a scene of indescribable Celtic excitement. It was a victory fair and square, and had nothing of the nature of a fluke about it. Indeed, it is not too much to say that on the afternoon's play the Welshmen were more than three points the better team. They deserved to win through their superior excellence in every department of the game; and those steadfast Cymric hearts which quailed not

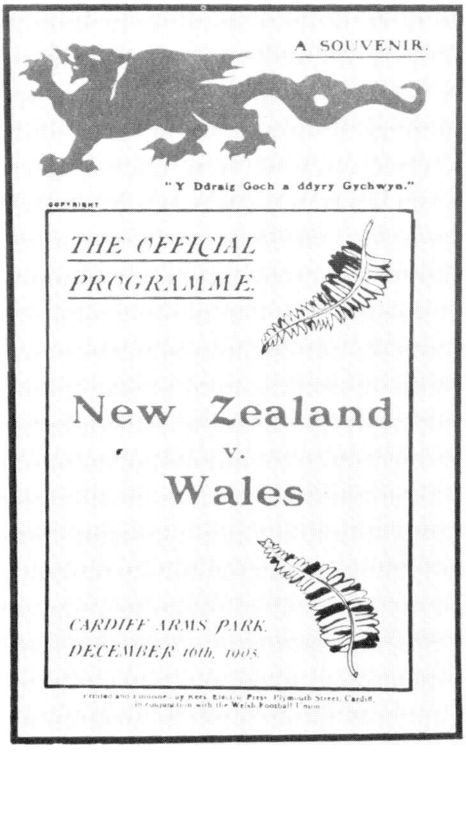

through all the long run of unbroken 'All Blacks' successes, disdaining the possibility of Welsh defeat, must now be glowing with rare pride and satisfaction.

The scene on the ground was an unparalleled one, even for a Welsh football match. As early as nine o'clock excited youths and men—some of whom had travelled all night from the remoter colliery districts—clamoured for admission at the gates. These were opened soon after ten, and by noon there was scarcely standing-room left. A vast sea of eager, excited fans packed tier upon tier some fifty or sixty deep, fringed the ground. From it there arose a continuous crackle of ardent Celtic chatter, broken every now and again by the deep, harmonious resonance of some patriotic refrain, which, started by a small knot here and there, was caught up on either side until the whole ground became enveloped in a noble volume of sound, perfect in rhythm and feeling, as from 40,000 trained choristers led by some invisible master baton. An entirely different crowd from the crowds that witnessed the defeat of England and Scotland and Ireland. Full of fire and enthusiasm, with only one thought—the thought of victory. A fervent, almost frenzied crowd, which drowned the bare suggestion of defeat in unreasoning burst of triumphant melody. This was the spirit which had carried the ancient Briton through many a hard-won fight against apparently impossible odds—this also was the Celtic answer to the seemingly invincible Colonial array before which all the world had bent the knee.

A famous English International said after the match: 'I don't think there is any team in the world, selected from all over the British Empire, that could beat Wales at Cardiff. They might beat them out of Wales, but there is something uncanny about a Cardiff crowd—a something that carries an invading fifteen off its balance. It may be the cheering, or it may be the singing, but there is a Celtic electricity in the air that, while it loosens our sinews and weakens our joints, has a marvellously astringent effect on the home team.'

This may or may not be true, but certain it is that the All Blacks seemed to be labouring under some strange, hypnotic influence from the moment they stepped on to the field. Even the usually awe-inspiring Maori war chant fell a little flat, and its remembrance was speedily engulfed in the crowd's inspiring, soulful response to the Welsh team's lead of *Land of Our Fathers*. There was a semi-religious, almost fanatical invocation in the fervour with which the vast assembly took up the strain: 'The land of my fathers! The land of the free!'

The All Blacks listened spellbound to the weirdly beautiful incantation and they never seemed quite able to shake off its effects while the game lasted.

The Welshmen sported the leek in their coats, but not in their hearts. Unlike most of the teams whom the All Blacks had vanquished, the Welsh fifteen entered the fray not to defend merely and keep the scoring down, but to meet thrust by thrust, guile by guile, combination by combination. They were not content merely to be passive spectators of the working of the hitherto irresistible New Zealand machinery. They meant to break it up—and break it up they did! The All Blacks' theory, openly proclaimed, is that the best form of defence is attack, and they had put it into practice with unmistakable success in twenty-seven previous encounters. But, unfortunately for them, the same view is held, and has been held for years, by Welsh footballers also. The inevitable consequence was that the two teams, about equal in experience, speed and weight, crashed together in a struggle wherein neither enjoyed any tactical advantage, except such as lies in the mere verbal distinction between 'five-eighths' and 'roving half'. The New Zealanders, lulled into a certain sense of false security by the previous effectiveness of their methods, scarcely dreamed that the same art and finesse which they employed would also be exerted by their opponents, added to the considerable advantage which the support of a Welsh crowds affords.

From the first minute it was easily perceptible that they had underestimated the Welshmen's fire and dash and resource. For the first time during their tour they were faced by men who had made up their minds to win, not merely to escape defeat by the smallest margin possible, as had been their experience in nearly every match they had hitherto played—men who knew nearly as much, if not quite as much, of the science of the game as they did themselves, and who, moreover, were as speedy, as strong, and as confident of the result. The machinery which had worked so smoothly in all their other matches now ceased to act. Every time the wheels began to move some quick, intelligent Welshman thrust in his spoke, and they ceased to revolve. In the first place, the Welsh forwards—a big, strong, clever pack—got the ball as often, if not more often, than their rivals. But even when Roberts did get it heeled out to him, and had started the mechanism—there was never any breakdown in that perfect scrum-half cog—the fatal defect appeared. Mynott, who received most of Roberts' passes, was, apparently, mesmerised by the crowd from the start, and it was a fateful decision which awarded him his place in preference to Stead. Though a player of great dash and speed, he was never Stead's equal for cleverness or judgement. But now he seemed to lose his head entirely. Times innumerable he mulled Roberts' passes, either dropping or knocking them on or passing them forward in the most juvenile fashion. He was flurried, oppressed by the shadow of Cliff Pritchard, the 'spoiler', whose mission it was to dislocate the five-eighths part of the machine, and thus put it out of gear. With a player of more resource than Mynott showed, this plan might have been circumvented. As it was, it succeeded admirably. The pivot of the New Zealand attack, the five-eighths, never got going at any point of the match, and, consequently, the whole machinery fell to pieces. Gwyn Nicholls, Cliff Pritchard and 'Dicky' Owen nipped nearly every movement in the bud. Not once did the New Zealand five-eighths and three-quarters succeed in 'cutting' their way through these past masters in the art of tackling. Every time they went for a man they stopped him. Nevertheless, Mynott, with a blind, reckless impetuosity born of success against weaker opponents, kept on trying to barge his way through a crowd of opponents, while his wing three-quarters stood impotently fuming, and Stead, carrying the touch-flag, looked unutterable things.

It was a hard, scrambling game for the most part—both sides wrought to the highest pitch of excitement—relieved by some bright flashes of Welsh passing, which, although not making much ground, nevertheless threw into bold relief the incapacity of their opponents in a department in which, although expected to shine, they failed most signally. There was scarcely a glimpse of the beautiful precision among the backs that had spread devastation throughout England, Ireland and Scotland.

Gallaher, who was early in trouble with the referee, received no mercy either from his opponents or the spectators. Indeed, the latter were most unfair to him. Throughout the game he was subjected to a pitiless fusillade of epithets which, to anyone save a man who, like Gallaher, has had the hardening experience of actual warfare—the New Zealand captain went through the South African campaign as a scout—must have been disconcerting to a degree.

But though Gallaher kept cool under provoking circumstances, many others of the team were visibly upset, and an air of nervousness seemed to pervade the ranks. Not only Mynott, but Hunter and Deans, usually so safe, failed to take or give passes time after time, and that

R. G. Deans, who was convinced he scored for New Zealand

Loose play, 1905

with no opponent near them. While as for Gillett, the full-back, he appeared almost unnerved, as if the greatness of the occasion were too much for him. And the more hesitating and anxious the All Blacks grew, the more confident and daring became the attacks of the Welshmen, urged on by the frantic cries of the crowd. Of a truth, the Cymric *hwyl* was working well!

Things were in this state when Owen got possession in the New Zealand '25' and, drawing the defence to the right by a superb feint, threw a long, high pass back to Cliff Pritchard, who passed to Gabe, who in turn transferred to Morgan for that speedy winger to race down the left touchline, and, evading Gillett's tackle, ground the ball just over the goal line. Wales had scored a try—as it turned out, the only score of the match—and for a few minutes it seemed as if every throat in the Principality, from Orme's Head to Milford Haven, was celebrating the event. Every one of the 45,000 Celts gave full rein to his passionate temperament. Sedate-looking men screamed themselves hoarse in incoherent ecstasy, while the more excitable preened and spluttered themselves purple in inarticulate spasms of frenzied delight. Wales had scored a try! Wales was winning!! Wales would win!!!

This was twenty-three minutes from the start, and the battle was renewed with undiminished vigour, with Wales still holding the upper hand. They had the best of it in the scrum; at back, Winfield was kicking superbly into touch, making fifty or sixty yards every time, saving his own forwards and running the other pack off their legs. A finer exhibition of clean fielding and safe kicking—in marked contrast to the Colonial full-back's work—has never been seen, considering the importance of the occasion, and Wales owes much of her victory to Winfield's faultless display.

The teams turned round with the All Blacks three points down—not very much to worry a team to whom three points every five minutes had been for months their normal rate of scoring. But now three points seemed to assume the magnitude of thirty. As the minutes slipped by, and no score came—nor looked like coming—the thrust with which Morgan had pierced their armour assumed serious proportions. Though 'not so deep as a well, nor so wide as a church door', it began to look as if, after all, it would be enough—would serve to make all the difference between victory and defeat. And so it proved. Strive though they did with might and main, they could not cross the Welsh line, which was defended as bravely and as tenaciously as the Britons of old held their fastnesses against Roman and Saxon assault. Time after time the All Blacks hosts surged right up to the Welsh line, but never quite got over, though time after time Welsh hearts leapt to their throats in agonised fear that they would. Once Roberts, who headed fierce attack on attack, was pulled down only inches from the line, and from one corner flag to the other there ensued a series of wild bullies and scrums that threatened disaster every minute to the defence. But still no score came. Again and again the Welshmen—particularly Nicholls and Winfield—raised the siege.

It was now that Wallace, chafing under the prolonged inaction which the Colonial three-quarter line had endured, rushed with the desperation born of despair into the thick of the fray. Gathering the ball from an opponent's toe, he tore his way through every obstacle, and in a trice was speeding down the field, with Deans on his flank, and only two opponents to pass. It looked an absolutely certain try. Winfield went for Wallace a dozen yards from the line, but 'ere he could reach

'Carbine' Wallace, who scored 230 points on the tour

him the ball had been passed out to Deans racing down the touchline. He, too, was collared, but not before he grounded across the Welsh line, though the referee—whose decision is bound to be accepted in such matters—declared that he had been 'held up', and ordered a scrum instead of a place-kick.

In a few more minutes the end came, and, amid another indescribable scene of wild enthusiasm, the victors were hoisted on to the shoulders of the jubilant crowd and carried to the dressing-room. The enclosure echoed for several minutes afterwards with the exuberant cheers of the triumphant Welshmen, and thousands of waving hats and fluttering handkerchiefs kept up the rejoicings long after vocal resources had been exhausted.

It has long been the contention of competent Welsh critics that the supremacy gained by the Principality at rugby football has been as much due to the fine work of their forwards as to the combination and cleverness of their backs. This theory received ample proof, as it was her forwards whom Wales had mainly to thank for her victory. For the first time since their arrival in this country the New Zealand pack found themselves beaten for cleverness in the scrum. The Scottish and Irish matches had shown that the New Zealand forwards were not invincible, but then both the Scottish and Irish forwards played their traditional game of wheeling or carrying the scrums, and in the art of heeling and setting their backs in motion showed themselves decidedly inferior to the All Blacks. This, however, is not the Welsh method of attack. Their forwards, though clever enough with their feet in the loose when the occasion demands it, play very much the same style of game as the New Zealanders in that they regard the scrum as an integral part of a piece of machinery, of no value without the aid of the backs to clinch home the attack.

> On the New Zealand side all the forwards played well, but, for once in a way, met a pack as heavy and skilful as themselves. Roberts, at half-back, was as skilful as ever in getting possession of the ball, and it was certainly not his fault that the New Zealand backs did not make any use of numberless opportunities.

This was not the end of the matter, of course, and the game, like almost every game with New Zealand since, was fraught with controversy. Deans believed he had scored and sent a telegram to the *Daily Mail* on the following day to assert his claim. In his memoirs, 'Carbine' Wallace asserted that it was Owen who had picked up the ball and replaced it

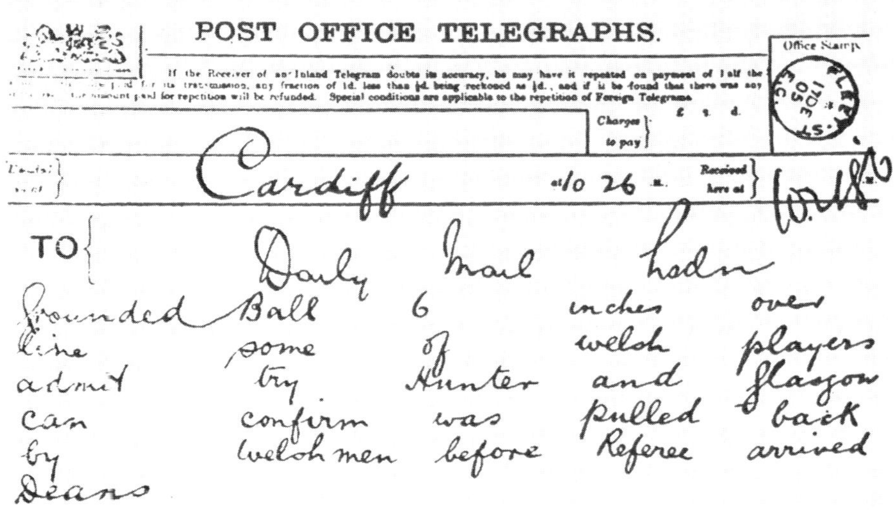
POST OFFICE TELEGRAPHS.

Cardiff

TO Daily Mail hadn grounded Ball 6 inches over line some of welsh players admit try Hunter and Glasgow can confirm was pulled back by Welshmen before Referee arrived Deans

Facsimile of the telegram sent to the *Daily Mail* by Bob Deans—his allegation that he was 'pulled back by Welshmen' is at variance with Wallace's story

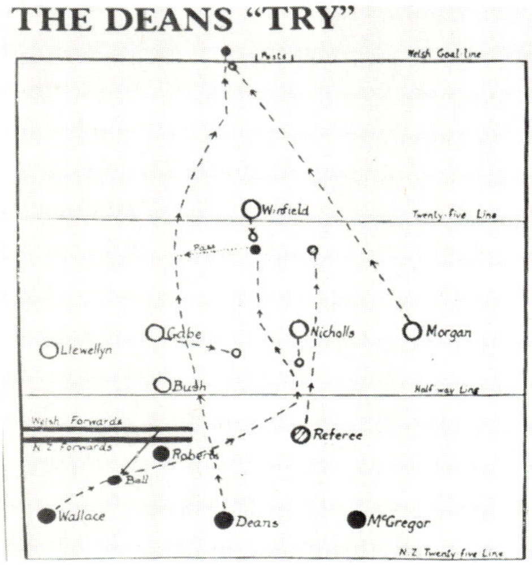

Wallace's diagram of Deans' try. Note ball grounded over line and position of referee, but where was Owen who allegedly picked up the ball and deposited it in the field of play?

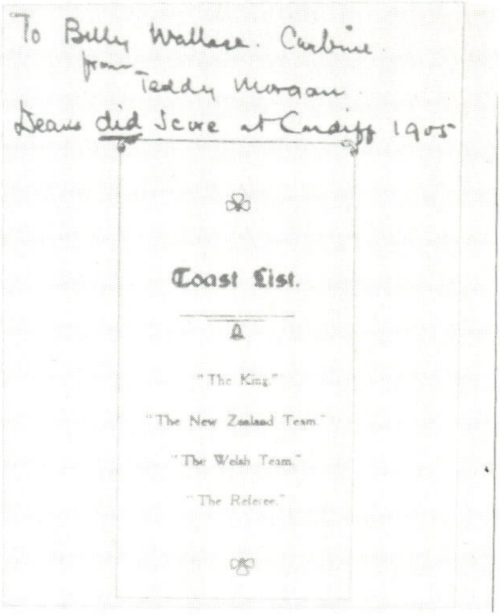

right, Toast list for dinner following New Zealand v. Wales match of 1924. Morgan wrote the message to Wallace on Cliff Porter's card.

just short of the line, telling the referee that Deans had 'forced the ball', later recalling that the crowd was silent, believing a try had been scored, whereas they would certainly have applauded a successful tackle. The referee, Mr Dallas of Scotland, never wavered in his conviction that a try had not been scored and told Bill Travers years later that he had examined the elbows of Deans' jersey to see if there were any marks of the white lime used to denote the try line, but there were none. George Nicholson, the New Zealand touch judge who had just taken over from Bill Stead and who felt the 'call of nature', ran parallel to Deans and was sure a try was scored, and the controversy was added to years later when Dr Teddy Morgan sent a message back to Wallace on a menu card, stating his belief that the try had been scored. The Welsh touch judge, Ack Llewellyn, also believed it was a try and in 1921, Morgan stated that when he first tackled Deans, he distinctly saw the white goal line underneath him.

We shall never know exactly what happened and probably no rugby match has been more discussed, but what is certain is that the solitary defeat of the New Zealand side on that tour established the game in Wales in a way that could hardly have been foreseen thirty years before.

There were, of course, incidents, as W. J. Townsend Collins wrote:

'The very air was charged with emotion. Hopes and fears were blended in an aching, choking anxiety. What the crowd felt was communicated to the players, and in the opening minutes they were so wrought that finish went to the winds. Most of the play at first was with the forwards, and it seemed as if both packs were determined to see how much punishment (within, or a little beyond the laws) their opponents could survive. No quarter was given by either side. Men were toppled over like ninepins—flung aside, dashed to the ground.'

In the *Western Mail*, it was reported, 'A New Zealand forward charged at Owen with swinging fist, but the 'Little Wonder' was not only unhurt, but laughing, and the crowd's growls changed to laughs.'

Welsh transgressions were not reported in the Welsh Press, but since the hard man of the Welsh pack, Dai 'Tarw' Jones, was not a man to lie down it is highly unlikely that none occurred. Like so many players of this era, little is known about him except the local legends which persist, and it is said of him that he once, after solemnly removing his tunic, forcibly ejected an Inspector from the police station in which he was

Dai 'Tarw' Jones ejecting an Inspector from Treherbert police station, having first removed his tunic

serving, and on another occasion was once disciplined for selling raffle tickets on duty.

Perhaps the two captains should have the last word. Said Dave Gallaher, 'It was a real good game, played out to the bitter end with the result that the better team won.' And Gwyn Nicholls: 'There was really nothing between the teams. The real difference appeared to be that we took advantage of our only opportunity to score.'

In the recollections of those who saw that game Arthur Gould makes one of his last appearances, dancing in ecstasy upon the Press table. He,

"Humpty Dumpty Had a Great Fall"

like his fellow selectors, was to have other joys, for this match came in the middle of the first Welsh golden era between 1900 and 1911 when Wales played forty-three matches against other countries, losing only seven, and only once at home to South Africa whom we have never beaten. It was this famous game against the All Blacks and this period of supremacy which led to a bank of memory whose collateral was the great players who had etched their names on the ledger. In these years another principle was born, and with it a famous exception. It was not whether Wales won that mattered (save perhaps against New Zealand!) but how Wales won, so that there was added a new dimension of Welsh expectations which had to last through some gloomy days when England at last recovered from the loss of the northern clubs and re-established herself in the days of W. J. A. Davies and Wavell Wakefield between 1912 and 1924. It was as if the economic fortunes of Wales were reflected in the performance of her national rugby team, for bleak years were to follow. The word depression came into the language and for the most part, until the arrival of the products of the universities and the county schools once more in the 1930s, all that the rugby fans had to sustain them were brief glimpses of the past brought to life by those players who retained the classic style. Thus a template was forged which has lasted ever since.

Phil Bennett after a day of triumph, Llanelli v. New Zealand, 1972.

3

The Template

This idea of a template is perhaps best understood by asking ourselves what characteristics have been displayed by Welsh sides which are special to them and whether the ingredients for victory are related to events outside the composition of the national side. We have certainly always done better when we have had a booming economy and national success has always followed the individual success of one or two clubs. A particular group of players playing regularly for a club at any given time has brought what Gould called the merits of combination to the national side, and it is probably no accident that great clubs like Cardiff and Newport had an influence on the national style of play in the immediate post-war period. The same was true of the London Welsh in the mid 1960s when the determination to make use of an attacking full-back was matched by a concentration of effort in winning loose ball from broken play with the idea of attacking from unexpected situations at every possible opportunity.

At the beginning of every golden era, this combination of the dominant club and the presence of one or two great players in that club or elsewhere is a pattern which repeats itself and the post-war Cardiff side, first captained by Jack Matthews, was associated with a style of rugby which was distinctive and free of the claustrophobic tensions which are sometimes apparent today. There was a philosophy of getting the ball to the wings early on in the game, and above all, a commitment to open-running football by the whole side. At the heart of its success was the Cardiff pack led by W. E. Tamplin which achieved a kind of undeserved anonymity; it provided opportunities galore which were so capitalised upon that the fame of the three-quarters overshadowed the essential ball-winning capacities of the forwards. This was county school football come to fruition and in the centre of it, literally, stood Bleddyn Williams, the most accomplished player most of us have seen.

Strongly built, a fine tackler and passer of the ball, he fits the description of Arthur Gould to a tee, and he was also capable of sidestepping off either foot, a man of all the talents in all weathers with a complete unselfishness and imperturbability that made his play classical. There are great players like (his contemporary) Lewis Jones,

Bleddyn Williams (Cardiff, Wales and the British Lions), a great centre with a Rolls-Royce imperturbability. 'Give the ball to Bleddyn!' the crowds used to shout, expecting and often getting miracles. Wales never lost when he was captain.

who have particular characteristics which remain in the memory. Jones had a mesmeric capacity for creating unorthodox movements, at times displaying a kind of brooding insolence which erupted into a dazzling run that you felt was his own special way of relieving his boredom in a drab game. Williams could remain unnoticed for whole periods of the game, however, coming to life when the occasion demanded his expertise and then demonstrating all the grace and style with which he is forever associated. He was also totally unselfish, a superb creator for others, and indeed his family, like that of the Travers family of Newport, are part of Welsh rugby history. Both Lewis Jones and Bleddyn Williams must rank with Gould or Albert Jenkins of Llanelli as men who cast a Welsh shadow over their contemporaries in the greater rugby world, and it is not surprising that some of them were often played out of position because the selectors, as well as the crowds, felt they could do anything.

It is not so, of course, and nowhere is this fallacy more clearly demonstrated than in the half-back positions where the Welsh

In Welsh rugby, half-backs are either quick or dead . . .
left, The quick: Cliff Jones through against Scotland, 1935
below left, Protected: Gareth Davies with J. P. R. Williams in attendance
below right, Caught: Gareth Edwards—for once!

contribution to the game has been unique. Here are the real specialists and it is again no accident that three men dominate in the scrum-half position in our most successful decades, all long-serving and all long-passing. It is as if the fire starts here with the all-important match to make the blaze, and at the root of the success of men like Dickie Owen, Haydn Tanner and Gareth Edwards another common factor emerges, the very quality which Gould spoke about—a supreme confidence, an arrogance even that made them stand out amongst their fellows so that time after time they picked themselves for the Welsh team, earning over a hundred international caps with a record of consistency that is staggering. They cannot, you feel, be ordinary men and indeed, thinking about them, it is not long before you set one against the other, and although Edwards' performances are fresh in the mind and will stand forever on film, it is just as well to remember that he was often contained by New Zealand's Sydney Going. I never saw Tanner so contained, in fact, never in any position when he was other than dominant. His career, interrupted by the war, began as a schoolboy with his cousin Willie Davies when they formed a famous partnership together at half-back for Swansea against the 1935 All Blacks.

Haydn Tanner

Two men dominate the last fifty years of Welsh rugby football, Haydn Tanner and Gareth Edwards. At times, both had the chilling stillness of executioners and an arrogance that belonged to the great duellists, with a touch of the Laurence Oliviers when they were tempted to do too much.
above left, Haydn Tanner
above right and below, Gareth Edwards

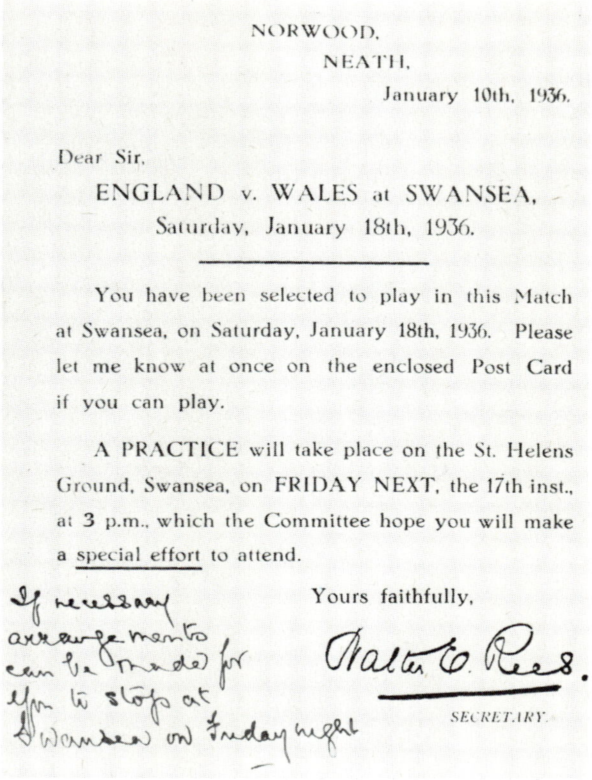

NORWOOD,
NEATH,
January 10th, 1936.

Dear Sir,

ENGLAND v. WALES at SWANSEA,
Saturday, January 18th, 1936.

You have been selected to play in this Match at Swansea, on Saturday, January 18th, 1936. Please let me know at once on the enclosed Post Card if you can play.

A PRACTICE will take place on the St. Helens Ground, Swansea, on FRIDAY NEXT, the 17th inst., at 3 p.m., which the Committee hope you will make a special effort to attend.

Yours faithfully,

Walter E. Rees.
SECRETARY.

If necessary arrangements can be made for you to stop at Swansea on Friday night

This was one of two occasions when schoolboys were blooded in senior football at the age of eighteen, and Swansea's victory that day, and later a Welsh victory against New Zealand when Tanner was paired with Cliff Jones, occurred at the very beginning of Tanner's career as if he were already following the old show business maxim—'Start big and build from there!' This quality of confidence shone through everything he did and, like Edwards, he stands in the golden landscape of rugby memory with all the flourish and swagger of an Italian bravo. Both were mercurial giants of athleticism about whom all who have seen them might debate for ever. You might say that proper comparison is bound to be artificial. There have been, for one thing, changes in the rules, coupled with the absence in Edwards' day of

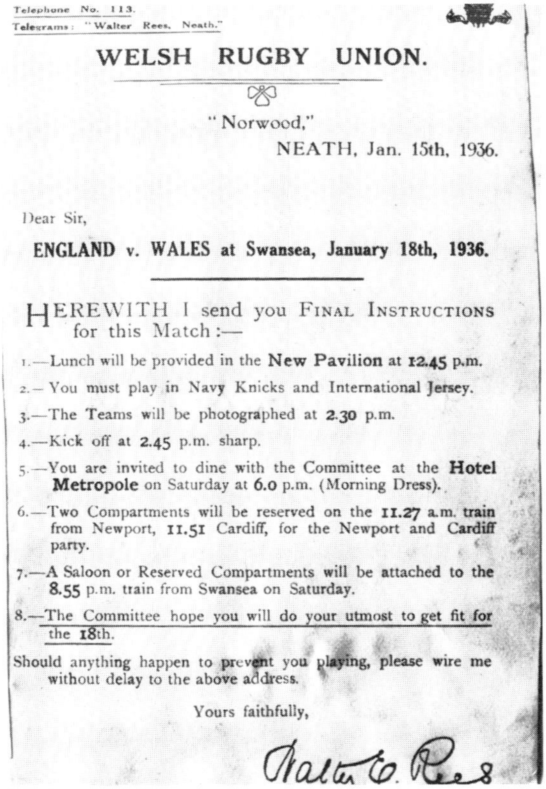

Telephone No. 113.
Telegrams: "Walter Rees, Neath."

WELSH RUGBY UNION.

"Norwood,"
NEATH, Jan. 15th, 1936.

Dear Sir,

ENGLAND v. WALES at Swansea, January 18th, 1936.

HEREWITH I send you FINAL INSTRUCTIONS for this Match:—

1.—Lunch will be provided in the **New Pavilion at 12.45** p.m.

2.—You must play in Navy Knicks and International Jersey.

3.—The Teams will be photographed at **2.30** p.m.

4.—Kick off at **2.45** p.m. sharp.

5.—You are invited to dine with the Committee at the **Hotel Metropole** on Saturday at **6.0** p.m. (Morning Dress).

6.—Two Compartments will be reserved on the **11.27** a.m. train from Newport, **11.51** Cardiff, for the Newport and Cardiff party.

7.—A Saloon or Reserved Compartments will be attached to the **8.55** p.m. train from Swansea on Saturday.

8.—The Committee hope you will do your utmost to get fit for the **18**th.

Should anything happen to prevent you playing, please wire me without delay to the above address.

Yours faithfully,

Walter E. Rees

the Tsarist terror wing-forwards who were on the prowl in Tanner's day, men like Ray Cale of Pontypool, or W. I. D. Elliot of Scotland, or D. F. White of Northampton who collected scalps on the very edge of the scalping laws. The most frightening rugby player I ever saw was Ray Cale who always seemed to be a Dostoevskian figure, the archetypal Imperial Russian policeman with that oddly long, flapping hair of his, the glazed eyes and the ominous watchful stance as he stood salivating thoughtfully on point duty at the end of the line-out. Although I never saw him involved in any illegality, the threat of his arrival on the scene was somehow more terrifying than the presence of any other wing-forward of his day, and he gave you the impression that when he apprehended, he arrested, prosecuted, adjudicated, convicted and sentenced—the complete destructive forward who dominated club football for a season or two. His seven caps were a meagre total for such a player, and no satisfactory explanation was ever given for his not being taken to New Zealand with the Lions.

There were others with whom Tanner had to cope, making comparison with Edwards difficult, but it is just as well to remember exactly what they did have in common, including a touch of the Laurence Oliviers when their partners did not call the shots. Their individual performances were on occasions so top-heavy with the weight of their immense talents that, like overbearing leading men, they unbalanced the supporting casts. Both won matches on their own, however, both could kick with either foot, playing dry day football when up to their knees in mud, and both gave off a quality that does not belong on the rugby field at all, an extra dimension that moves above confidence to the arrogance of the great duellists. Tanner had the height and the reach, Edwards was nearer the ground and could scoop better—he was probably the more talented offensive kicker with perhaps a little more time to move in the game of his day. Edwards says he taught himself to spin pass after the manner of Chris Laidlaw but there does not seem to be a time when Tanner learned anything, and on the break there was little between them, both having an unflurried coldness of purpose and the determination to go alone which sometimes made you feel that regiments could not have stopped them. Perhaps it is the length and speed of pass which makes Edwards and Tanner stand out, and, as a natural consequence, the all-important space which they created for their partners to perform their own wizardries.

Over the years, there have been other scrum-halves who have formed a type. If Edwards and Tanner are the aristocrats who do everything a little better with greater certainty and more style, there have been others who fall into equally desirable categories. They are the perfect servants like Wynford Davies, W. J. Darch, Handel Greville, Rex Willis, 'Chico' Hopkins, Selwyn Williams and Clive Shell, usually of a smaller build but compact still, arch schemers on their day who ferret at the feet of forwards like snapping terriers. There are others like

left, Rex Willis of Cardiff whose combination with Cliff Morgan created the most effective partnership until Edwards linked with Barry John
below, Ray 'Chico' Hopkins of Llanelli, 1972

right, Selwyn Williams as a schoolboy
below left and right, and opposite: Clive Shell of Aberavon whose technical efficiency on his day was as perfect as a superbly lubricated machine

Onllwyn Brace and Clive Rowlands who were such great individualists that they fall into a special category of their own. I call these the thinking players with a touch of the gambler about them, three-card brag men all. Sometimes they are wanderers, moving from club to club in search of a partner, always they have a strong individuality of play and can be looked upon to produce rabbits out of hats. When you think of them, you do not automatically think of their partners and they are not associated with partnerships. It is natural to talk of Tanner and Davies, Willis and Morgan, or Edwards and John, but both

Brace, 'the bag of tricks'

Onllwyn Brace and Clive Rowlands are odd men out, and it is hard to remember games in which they played when they created opportunities for their partners to shine more than they did themselves. It is as if some players, born out of their time, were never to make a half-back marriage that can rank with the famous partnerships. Brace, like Haydn Tanner a product of Gowerton grammar school, sometimes played at outside-half and represented Aberavon, Newport, Llanelli, Swansea and Oxford University before captaining Wales, his most successful partnership being at club level with Newport's Roy Burnett.

Roy Burnett of Newport, described as 'four-footed' and 'Twinkletoes'. Like Morgan, he gave a touch of character to the game but was awarded only one cap against England in 1953.

Colin Meads advances on Clive Rowlands who is about to make a mark, Wales v. New Zealand 1963

Rowlands is laid out and the penalty is awarded.

Brace was a bag of tricks, a schemer who thought about the game deeply, and as a player he was often in competition with Cardiff's Lloyd Williams who was a scrum-half in the ninth forward category. The other distinctive player who has probably had the most influence on Welsh play since the war is Clive Rowlands of Pontypool and Swansea. Far from being a classical player Rowlands was the ugly duckling, a man of his era who adapted himself to meet a period of stalemate, a tactical general and a virtuoso bad-weather player who would not be beaten. Never princely, he was an artisan who could kick a ball upon a sixpence and there was about him—in club and international games—a

doggedness that represented a very special quality of Welsh rugby. If we revere the elegance of a graceful runner and place a special emphasis upon fleetness of foot, the thief-in-the-night quality of a Barry John, or the Rolls-Royce imperturbability of a great centre like Bleddyn Williams, we are usually admiring such players for qualities which are rarely seen, which we certainly do not possess ourselves and which are not a part of the environment in which we live. We know little of elegance and grace in an environmental sense and our reverence for special players springs perhaps from our deprivation. Thus the heroes of the depression were wizards like Cliff Jones, the long striding juggernauts like Wilf Wooller, the crash tacklers like Claude Davey, or the laconic kickers like Vivian Jenkins, all of whom presented a coolness and confidence and a richness of talent, qualities that were manifestly

Vivian Jenkins

not present in the society which surrounded them. These players and others like them were thus untypical and somehow unrepresentative of the world of their admirers but conversely, there was something about Clive Rowlands having himself a hard afternoon behind a begrimed pack in the pouring rain that was a reflection of ourselves and our immediate past. If Barry John played in the aura of royal robes, Clive Rowlands never lost his artisan's dungarees, but there was never a game when he did not give his all, and the sight of him working the touchline Saturday after Saturday represented the bread and butter of Welsh club football. While we have exhausted ourselves with praise for Gareth Edwards, Rowlands stands out in the memory as a workman whose confidence, aggression and guile raised him above the level of his fellows by an attitude of mind that was reflected in his scowling countenance as clearly as a conviction of sin might implant itself on the face of a country preacher. Many great players play in the warm adulation of crowds. Not so Rowlands whose critics followed him in equal proportion to his admirers. I have an abiding memory of him playing one of his last games for Swansea against Cardiff, luring the Cardiff wing-forwards offside by a feint, securing a winning penalty and drawing an appreciative chuckle from the knowledgeable along the terraces. Like Cliff Morgan whose range of facial expressions resembled that of an opera singer at La Scala, especially if he were late tackled, you could sometimes read a game on Rowlands' face, and even if he had not—as coach—become one of the architects of the success of the next decade of Welsh rugby football, he would still have written his name on the ledger, albeit with a kicking boot, a tommy box and a workman's jack beside it, symbols of a dour style of play which has nothing to commend it but courage and success. They called him 'Topcat', and 'Topcat' he was, a leader of the Welsh team to their first victory in Edinburgh for ten years, and of the first Triple Crown side for thirteen years, a Horatio who held the bridge.

Rowlands, like others, thinks that the Australian dispensation law introduced to penalise direct kicking to touch between the 25s changed the nature of the game which he played, but half-back combinations had been successful long before; and when we come to consider the role

'Topcat' Rowlands

of the fly-half, there is no doubt that the Welsh fly-half position has always been a key role, the most discussed and debated, the most difficult to fill, and at the same time the crowning jewel of the Welsh ensemble since the game began. Just why we should develop players who are superb in this position remains a mystery. We are told that in the very beginning of the game half-backs rarely worked as pairs, and that they were generally servants of the packs in front of them. The first most successful specialisation in the Welsh team probably came under Gould's captaincy when Percy Phillips and Fred Parfitt of Newport played at half, Parfitt's expertise at passing securing the scrum-half berth for himself while Phillips became one of the first specialised runners with the ball. Thereafter the division remained. Percy Bush of

Cardiff was another who began the parade, and indeed the debate as to which partner was most suitable for him. This was to be repeated and before the Second World War there began an argument which was to arise endlessly over the merits of two of Wales' most famous fly-halves, Cliff Jones of Cardiff and Willie Davies of Swansea. Both partnered Tanner and both were match winners, and it seems that the elusive running and body swerve of Davies was in contention against the sudden acceleration and sidestepping of Cliff Jones who was certainly the most publicised player of his day. They, like all those before and after them, fell into categories and from the beginning there seems to have been a difference both in style and in temperament. There is the natural instinctive runner and the 'made' player whose effort appears greater, who in some ways is more exciting to watch since he is a duellist and brings a conscious act of deception to bear when beating a man. On the one hand there is grace, the nervous intuitive instincts of a

Haydn Tanner and Willie Davies seen here playing for Swansea. When they played against New Zealand in 1935, the New Zealand Captain, Jack Manchester, complained when defeat was imminent: 'This can't happen to us.' The All Blacks thought the partnership 'touched by glory'.

Cliff Jones with Haydn Tanner (*seated on ground, left and right*)

sleek and darting forest animal; on the other there is a mental calculation and usually a greater point of identification and admiration. The sidestepper at his best gives off a kind of 'Look, no hands!' attitude. One has a cool, insouciant grace, the other is wound up like a spring. One deceives, the other humiliates. This first group I call the High Church outside-halves, the second, the Chapel outside-halves. The greatest of these since the war was Cliff Morgan who looked as if he worried and who often seemed as if he were playing fifteen men on his own. Of course, the categories are not as clear-cut as that, and no player in this position can be fully considered without an assessment of his defensive abilities. The qualities can sometimes overlap so that some fly-halves become non-denominational, but the distinction is there and always seems to have been present.

As to why Wales produces more fly-halves of quality than any other country, the answer must lie in tradition. Most small children who grow up in a rugby environment tend to hear tales about famous players of the past, and fly-halves figure most conspicuously in the legend-making; then again, the position is certainly the most glamorous in the sense that it lends itself to crucial decision-making. Here the match can be won or lost. Here stands the commanding general. From this position, tactics can be dictated. When there is a gain line to be broken, one break will suffice, and a match can be won or lost in a second, but even with the modern concept of fifteen-man rugby where all are piano-players, the fly-half position remains crucial since he is the principal distributor and must know when to pass and when to kick. My own view is that this glamour has lessened somewhat since the advent of the fifteen-man game and we seldom see a fly-half beating a man from set-piece situations as we used to. It also seems to be that the

Outside-halves, more properly described as 'fly', fall into two categories: the High Churchmen and the Chapel outside-halves. *below*, Glyn Davies, a High Churchman, in action against England, 1949

More High Churchmen . . . *above*, Barry John *below left*, David Richards *below right*, Cliff Morgan, a Chapel outside-half whose range of facial expressions resembled an opera singer's at La Scala. Sometimes he seemed to be playing whole teams on his own.

speed of taking a pass on the burst has diminished with the result that the fly-half to fly-half contest has changed, but for all these nuances which increase the game as a spectacle by involving all the players, the importance of the position remains.

This still does not fully answer the question as to why Wales produces so many halves, and some believe that it is a question both of topography and build. So many fly-halves come from the Welsh valleys where from infancy they live crowded lives in busy streets, and Cliff Jones relates that from the moment his mother let him out of the front door as a small child, he was constantly at risk. 'I found myself on the only road up the valley which was teeming with traffic . . . you had a pair of tramlines, you had to avoid the tramcars, or the lorries or the pushbikes, and when you crossed the road, you came to the railway line, and if you were lucky enough to cross the railway line and reach safety, you fell into the river!' Cliff Morgan relates that before he was allowed to play at outside-half his school sportsmaster acually took out a tape measure and measured his legs! There was a limit, it seems, and openings could not be profitably used by the long-legged. Most players begin their playing lives with an image of a player they want to emulate and in some cases they know about the player before they have even seen him. What is interesting is that from the start the halo is cast in the mind of the listener. Thus legend breeds legend and perhaps it is part of the mystique that Cliff Morgan stood as a little boy in a room full of souvenirs belonging to his predecessor Cliff Jones, who in turn relates that even as a small child he heard his father talk of Percy Bush, another Rhondda player. When he was playing soccer as a primary schoolboy he was also aware of Windsor Lewis, the Cambridge fly-half, even though he had not seen him. Thus the lore was present before the performance although Jones was a soccer supporter at the time of Cardiff City's heyday. He did not begin playing rugby football until he went to secondary school, moving from the School XV to a representative side, Penygraig and District. But the crucial influence came when he went to Llandovery College where, like many future players, he came under the spell of T. P. Williams, who had what Jones describes as 'the nearest approach to the fundamental principles of

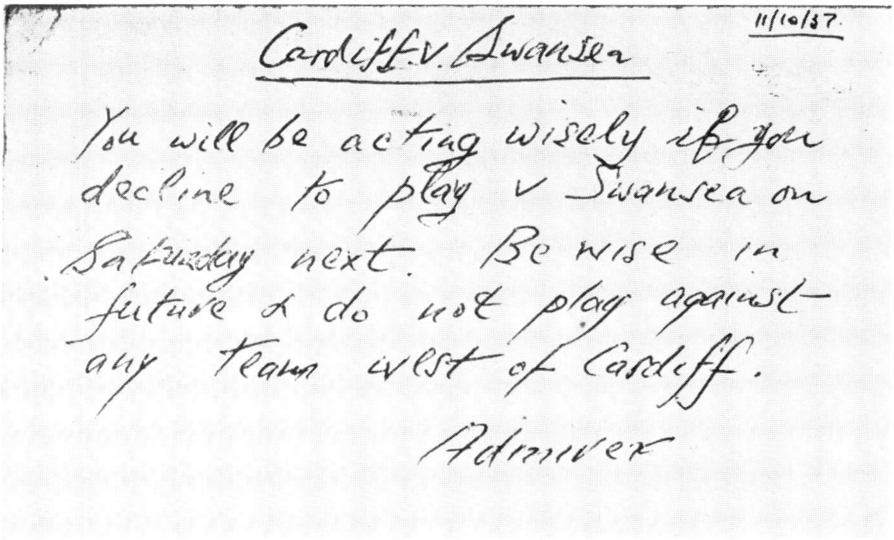
11/10/37.

Cardiff v. Swansea

You will be acting wisely if you decline to play v Swansea on Saturday next. Be wise in future & do not play against any team west of Cardiff.

Admirer

An anonymous postcard sent to Cliff Jones before the Cardiff-Swansea game, 1937

rugby football as demonstrated by the New Zealanders, especially insisting on the value of possession from the loose'. Here at Llandovery College, coaching began in earnest for Cliff Jones. He was out almost every day with a half-back partner, 'taking passes in all positions, down at your feet, above your head, in all weathers . . . He'd train me to a speed off the mark—just like a pony in a circus at the end of a long bridle. He'd have me running around him and he'd put the ball further and further in front of me, making me stretch because he maintained that speed over fifteen yards was the greatest thing in rugby football.'

For Cliff Jones, as for other public schoolboys and university men of the period, coaching was an accepted part of the game which was not to be introduced to national or club sides with the same intensity for several decades. Although this did not reflect on the individual flair of three-quarters, in senior football the all-important possession of the ball was haphazard because Welsh forwards were not together as a pack. 'For a Welsh outside-half,' says Cliff Jones, 'Utopia was to be born a Welsh half-back and play behind a New Zealand pack.'

This state of affairs was to change and it began to do so perhaps after the war when the effect of the schoolboy footballers made its

Capt. Walter E. Rees, a one-time recruiting sergeant seen here escorting Cliff Jones off the field in 1936. He was first elected to the Welsh Rugby Union in 1889 and served as Secretary for 52 years.

impression on the rugby football which had been kept going throughout the war by one or two famous clubs, by service sides which allowed professionals to play with amateurs, and above all by the Welsh grammar schools, who produced the most distinctive half-backs and three-quarters of the next decade. Now the wheel had turned full circle and the grammar schools began to repeat the process begun by the public schools in the early years. Even before the war ended, running, jinking half-backs began to appear in profusion and the old debates began again. County school football was running football, forwards were servants of the backs, and there was fierce competition from other winter sports. But if you wanted to play soccer, you did so in youth clubs as few county schools encouraged anything but rugby football with the result that the school created its heroes in the rugby image and the winning of colours was accorded the same prestige as in the public schools. Most schools ran second fifteens and even a form of forty boys could raise a side, so most schools had a pool of players upon which to draw. Most of us explored South Wales as a consequence of playing for such teams, winding our way up neighbouring valleys or journeying to Cardiff where we played against half a dozen or so schools. The Welsh Secondary Schools XV was accorded all the status of the national side and the trials were a matter of intense interest. It is debatable whether or not these teams were intensively coached but every side travelled with a schoolmaster and, although training was encouraged, it did not amount to much more than a concern for physical fitness. There were men like T. P. Williams who were knowledgeable about their rugby but as for the improvement of skills, I have a feeling that it was left very much to individual players to improve themselves. There were no doctrinaire laws that stifled individual enterprise and excessive kicking was firmly disapproved of. The schoolmasters knew what they wanted and retained the image of the open game in their minds. The Welsh Secondary Schools team had been strong before the war and after it, players seemed to emerge with all the flair that was necessary to maintain interest in the game. It was a three-quarter dominated game and, as soon as the clubs began once more to return to their pre-war strength, there was a sudden explosion of talent leading to the dominance of a Cardiff fifteen which carried on the traditions of schoolboy football, making it one of the most attractive sides ever. Cardiff had been the scene of some wartime charity matches when professionals like Jim Sullivan of Wigan had played with amateur players, and the club restarted with a pool of players including Bleddyn Williams, Billy Cleaver and Jack Matthews, all products of Welsh secondary schools. Within a year the visit of the New Zealand army touring team, the Kiwis, was to restore a blend of magical elements that soon included a debate about fly-halves. It was as if nothing had ever changed.

* * *

The fly-half position is frequently the subject of ferocious argument, perhaps because we have a fixed image of a style at the back of our minds. The most heated debate since the war was over the respective merits of Glyn Davies and Billy Cleaver of Cardiff. *right*, Billy Cleaver—'the pre-computer kicker with the post-computer kick'

Two fly-halves dominated the period immediately after the war, Glyn Davies of Pontypridd and Billy Cleaver of Cardiff, and it has always seemed to me that the differences between them reflected styles of play which span the hundred years of Welsh rugby football. Both were fine players, both had markedly different characteristics, but Glyn Davies belonged to the past while Cleaver was a portent of the future. No one who saw them could fail to take up a position in favour of one or the other, and I had better say at the outset that as a contemporary of Glyn Davies I was so biased that any impartiality was impossible. From the beginning his career was to be cast in a heroic light, for he followed a sidestepping fly-half into a school team that was committed to an offensive three-quarter game and only lost two matches in five years, sometimes running up cricket scores with other players like Alan Goodfield, John Fry, John Llewellyn and Russell Dobbs who were all to be prolific scorers and shine in senior football. At the core of this team, the captain and scrum-half Wynford Davies had the long, immediate pass from the base of the scrum which, exceptional in a schoolboy, was the basis of the partnership. Thus, during the time he played as a schoolboy, Glyn Davies came to maturity with the certainty of quick possession that fly-halves thrive on and, as a result, did not have the slightest doubt about himself for the greater part of his schoolboy career. In many ways the school team was a forerunner of the Cardiff

Glyn Davies

team which emerged after the war in the sense that it, too, was committed to playing county school football, but where Billy Cleaver, several years his senior, had Bleddyn Williams alongside him,—the most dangerous centre of his era—Glyn Davies was himself cast in the Williams mould, capable of a break off either foot and with the same ability to penetrate the opposition. For Cleaver, it seems to me now, the role of midwife to Williams and Matthews was essential, whereas Glyn Davies, an attacker rather than a defender for most of his schoolboy career, came to the game with exactly the same attitude of mind which characterised the fly-halves of the early years of the game. He was there to distribute and to feed, but he was also there to scintillate on the breaks, a function which Cleaver left to Williams to perform. Davies' career was in the line of his pre-war predecessors, and he had that quality which marks all great players, the capacity to stand out over their fellows to such an extent that other positions do not carry quite the same importance. Watching him on the break, often beating two or three men, was the ultimate in excitement. Cleaver was to be admired for other things. Both he and Davies were good passers of the ball, but Cleaver was a tactical kicker who could break forwards' hearts, a man who was totally unselfish in play but did not have the ability to beat men with the same insolent grace as Davies.

I was present when Glyn and Wynford Davies were capped from school in the 'victory' internationals and although Wynford did not quite measure up to the hurly-burly of international football, Glyn demonstrated his elegant capabilities, beating the Scottish full-back K. I. Geddes at Swansea, luring him on the wrong foot and then side-stepping inside him in the classic manner. Injury kept him out of the next game against France when Cleaver played and thereafter there was a duel between the two men whenever the virtues of their respective styles were discussed. Cleaver often seemed to file forwards, pinning back the opposition down the touchline with his long raking kicks, resting his own pack and applying pressures which Williams and Matthews were to capitalise on. His kicking was the lynch-pin of his play and detractors wishing for another golden era called him Billy Kick. He was the pre-computer kicker with the post-computer kick

Wynford and Glyn Davies were picked for a Welsh team as schoolboys. The school naturally received a half day's holiday, and match reports were read aloud in the assembly hall.

and beside him, when you looked at Glyn Davies at his best, it was like comparing a poet with an accountant. It has to be said, however, that in close-fought games with destructive wing-forwards Cleaver was imperturbable, whereas the High Church outside-half is very dependent on the quality of his service. Although Glyn Davies sometimes succeeded brilliantly, as he did when he played with Haydn Tanner against England in 1949, he could also fail and was never the defender that Cleaver proved himself to be.

Glyn Davies's career was short, like that of Cliff Jones, as if fly-half play has some of the essence of art about it and is of necessity short-lived. Like a lyric poet, he could burn with a hard gem-like brilliance in a wonderous arc and then the flame would die. About the play of such men there is often a cool, disapproving arrogance that says, 'Lay not your hand upon me, felon!' and when a scintillating break comes off—rugby football becomes ecstatic. For all the attractions of fifteen-man rugby, this kind of brilliant individual player has not progressed in quite the same way and, to my mind, the only player of the present era who resembles Davies is David Richards of Swansea who has the same wicked acceleration over twenty yards but who, like others before him, has missed the regular service of a partner who can bring out all his talents. This is not to say that there have been no other fly-halves of top-drawer quality, but the speed off the mark and destructive incisiveness of the side-step when making the clean break is a rare gift, and indeed Richards, playing at centre for Wales, dropped a pass in the 1979 English international in a way that put me in mind of Jack Matthews, the Cardiff centre. He was accelerating at such a rate that you were forced to the conclusion that even the dropped passes of the great players were more exciting than the successes of the lesser. But the days of the individual duels have perhaps long been numbered and only rarely shall we see the past truly echoed. (On the subject of duels, I like the remark made by the mother of one of Cliff Morgan's rivals when he was bidding for his place in the Welsh team. 'Put the two of them in a field on their own with the ball and let them fight it out between them!')

After Cleaver came Cliff Morgan who waited in the wings during the post-war controversy and, in a bizarre way, might have been a product of both Cleaver and Davies. He was a stout defender with a coffin-nailing kick when required, a Chapel outside-half with a dynamic break and all the exciting qualities of his predecessors plus something extra of his own. Like Clive Rowlands later, there was something essentially South Walian about Morgan, and the sight of his hunched figure and often aggrieved stance as he waited with bowed head, or turned his mournful accusing stare on a late tackler, was for me half the pleasure of an afternoon.

The classic fly-halves like Glyn Davies or Barry John made everything look easy, whereas Morgan sometimes left you with the impression that he might have damaged himself in the process. But when the spring unwound it was just as dynamic, and on balance he was a more effective player than any of his predecessors, reaching heights on the hard dry grounds of South Africa which went unseen at home. Carwyn James, a High Churchman, was one of his rivals but they were never seriously in contention, for Morgan's partnership with Rex

Welsh captain Phil Bennett scores the first try for Wales, Wales v. England 1978

Willis was a perfect understanding and of all the half-back combinations since the war, this one must rate as the equal of any. Of all his successors David Watkins was most like him, equally effective on occasions but never quite achieving the rapport with a partner which Morgan did. Phil Bennett, as great a kicker as Cleaver on his day, was another amalgam of the talents. What is extraordinary is that such players appear again and again, each one bringing familiar traits, each one special, and when they achieve the rapport with a partner that brings the best out of both, games come alight as they have always done. Half-backs, more than any other position, have been touched by glory since the best of them have displayed that instinctive Welsh flair which makes our rugby football at its best so distinctive. You can value them for many things: for the way they beat men, for the way they link up with their three-quarters, for their incisive knowledge of the precise moment to kick or to pass, or for their saving graces in defence. Anyone who saw Phil Bennett's last kick in the famous match between Llanelli and the 1972 All Blacks will remember it with special pleasure, for Bennett has that air of frailty which is typical of many Welsh halves, and the sight of him driving back opponents twice his size is part of the real thrill of rugby football, the kind of contest which distinguishes it from any other game. That day, in a cauldron of endeavour, his role was that of a kicking half, placing his kicks to cause the utmost confusion, selecting a long penalty punt to hover over Grant Batty, the fiery New Zealand wing, seconds after he had come on to the field as a replacement, testing him in exactly the same way as he had tested Joe Karam, the young full-back, in the opening minutes of the game. The pressure was on from the beginning, and Bennett's boot was eloquent in attack and defence, his last forty-yard kick a clearance that capped a faultless performance of courage and skill, and which was enhanced by the service he got all afternoon from his partner 'Chico' Hopkins who played his finest game on that occasion. In a strange way, these partnerships where one partner dominates the other give more pleasure than when giants are paired, possibly because the sight of a small scrum-half giving his all is a greater test of the man than the effortless sophistication of a master. Bennett, like Cliff Morgan, played some of his best games on the hard, dry grounds of South Africa but unlike

The spare frame of Phil Bennett springs forward with the ball after one of his famous sidesteps.

One of the most famous partnerships of all, Gareth Edwards and Barry John. The length of the Edwards pass is clearly visible.

Morgan, his skills remain encapsulated on film. They both displayed at times the hunted, despairing quality which made their breaks all the more defiant—a reaction to circumstances which forced them to take control and seize initiatives from unusual positions. Both of them made things look more difficult than did Barry John who had an effortless style. Where Bennett worked, John glided, but both were splendid defensive players, finding in Edwards the kind of partner who gave them the room to move which would have made them superb in any era of the game. Edwards' greatest achievement was not just the massive stamp he could put on the game by his own crackerjack athleticism, but his decisive role in these two partnerships which blossomed both for Wales and two successful Lions tours to New Zealand and South Africa.

Behind them and every pair of half-backs there were always men who could capitalise on their speed. In every successful era there were three-quarters who added their own ingredients to the broth as well as ball-winners in front without whom they could never have flourished: here again a pattern has always shown itself. For every successful pairing there has flourished simultaneously a hooker who stood out amongst his fellows, and also a line-out combination which ensured clean and swift possession over and above what half-backs in evenly matched teams had a right to expect. Just as Edwards became a fixture in Welsh sides, so too did hookers like Bobby Windsor, Jeff Young, Dai Davies and Bryn Meredith, and earlier still Bill Travers who, like Haydn Tanner, played for Wales before and after the war. Their longevity in Welsh sides was matched by the third essential which has reappeared and made itself obvious, the presence of the line-out expert. Some, like Mervyn Davies, Delme Thomas and Alan Martin are fresh in the mind, whereas others like John Gwilliam and Roy John wrote their names large into the success of post-war sides. Others still like

Jeff Young (of Harrogate), one of Wales' long-serving hookers

above left and right, Jeff Young and Brian Price 'in the wars' at Lancaster Park, Christchurch, and Cardiff Arms Park
left Russell Robins of Pontypridd (whom the French considered the best forward in the world) and Clem Thomas of Swansea in action for the British Lions against Northern Transvaal

Rees Stephens, Rhys Williams, Brian Price and Alun Pask carved two accolades, one in the public eye and another from their opponents, becoming forwards' forwards, men whose contribution had another dimension that earned them a respect which lasted long after they finished playing. About them and their protectors there was often an anonymity, and their full presence was sometimes only appreciated when they were not playing and were sorely missed. Like Mervyn Davies, whose aim was to reduce all errors from his game, all the great forwards have a concept of efficiency at the heart of their play and, while the spectacular foragers and maulers remain in the memory, the principal result of squad training was an enlargement of this concept until we had an organised pattern of play. The result was an improvement in the quality of possession obtained, and we soon reached a technical age where the influence of coaching meant that we

'Rugby football has long ceased to be a game for those who can play pianos and those who can shift them.' The skills of the big men remain unchanged at club and international level.
Opposite page: above left, Bob Penberthy (Pontypridd); *above centre*, Alan Martin (Aberavon); *above right*, Brian Price (Newport); *below left*, Mervyn Davies (Swansea); *below centre*, Delme Thomas (Llanelli); *below right*, Roy John (Neath)
This page: Rees Stephens of Neath

'There are also forwards who stand out, men who receive two accolades, one in the public eye, the other amongst their contemporaries.'
above: Mervyn Davies, in the aftermath of a tackle.
right: 'Charlie' Faulkner's birthday try

above, Bryn Meredith (Newport) coming in to tackle
left, Alun Pask scores

depended less on the influence of the great players, though we were still glad to have them!

The template had not changed, but in the 1970s there was a coming together of all the talents which, aided by the changes in the laws and the creation of the squad system under a national coach, blossomed forth into the most spectacular era of all. We were now in the age of the superstar, and only New Zealand could claim superiority in a clutch of hard-fought games which avenged the most famous game of all. These games were, however, remarkable from the Welsh point of view in that one ingredient was missing, a demonstration of Welsh flair. With all the preparations and the intensity of coaching, it is ironic that previous victorious matches were always characterised by that genius who seized on the opportunity to make something out of nothing. It might be the bustling industry of Cliff Morgan, or Clem Thomas' brilliant cross kick in 1953, or Wilf Wooller's dummy scissors in 1935, but of late, while the excitement was always present, few could emulate

W. H. Clement, Secretary of the Welsh Rugby Union

left, Ray Williams, formerly Coaching Organiser, now Centenary Officer of the WRU
below, John Lloyd, Welsh Team Coach, 1980

John Dawes, the best passer of a ball of his era, captain and coach of Wales and the British Lions, and captain of the Barbarians against New Zealand in 1973, one of the most enjoyed games of the decade

Jack Manchester, the New Zealand captain's remark in 1935, 'I never played in such a thrilling game.' It was left to the Barbarians and the All Blacks to re-create that game in 1973, a game of all the talents when the result became secondary to the quality of play and when the adventurous approach of both teams made a nonsense of parochial considerations, an omen perhaps for the future. We provided the ground, the captain and some of the players, but the inspiration was with the Barbarians and a New Zealand team who forgot their cares after an arduous tour. More than a touch of glory, this game was all glory, and rugby football was the victor.

I see this famous game as a high watermark and a convenient point to remind myself that the traditional Barbarians fixture marking the end

above and below: Grant Batty of New Zealand displeased at being late-tackled by Tommy David of Pontypridd during the New Zealand v. Barbarians game, 1973

Sometimes the agony is on the board, not at five to four, but a few minutes later when Brian McKechnie of New Zealand kicked the winning penalty in the game between Wales and New Zealand in 1979

of an overseas tour is now always held at the Arms Park in Cardiff. We are the hosts, privileged ones at that, and our expectations of the players are probably greater than anywhere else in the world. On such occasions we free ourselves of our fierce loyalties and prepare for a spectacle which we usually get. At the same time, we are mindful that we are a Welsh crowd and like to think we know a thing or two! The total identification which we have with our national team is absent. We can relax and enjoy the game in the way in which it was meant to be enjoyed. It is not a time for partisan loyalties but for sheer delight, and when our visitors are the New Zealanders, for once we can view them dispassionately; and in this mood, it is as well to reflect how much we owe them.

Without New Zealand and that famous victory in 1905, our rugby history might have been different since it confirmed rugby football as our national game. Disputed try or no the kudos lasted, and more importantly, we have between us one thing in common: both countries have made the game available to all, irrespective of social class, and have never tolerated that exclusivity which precludes the mixing of all-comers. The paths we have taken stem from the way we have seized upon an English game and invested it with a role it was never intended to have. From the beginning we have expected our players to articulate our desires and represent us in a way that we are not represented in any other sphere. Since those early days, the word 'Welsh' has become synonymous with rugby football in the greater world for the simple reason that our contribution has been identifiable and different. It is, in essentials, exactly what it always has been, and while we have our faults and like Humpty Dumpty we can have an ignoble Twickenham fall from grace of our own making from time to time, we remain inheritors of a legacy of enthusiasm which still depends on the courage and skill of our players. Fortunately, these have never been lacking. Neither have we failed in the cultivation of the game at the grass roots with the result that for the rest of us, the pleasures remain.

I have tried to state some of them, to isolate the players that have pleased me, to trace some of the strands of the Welsh connection. To state your preference for a particular player or era is a part of these pleasures, as is the nursing of a sense of irredeemable loss when they pass away. They do not shout 'Give the ball to Bleddyn!' as they used to, expecting and getting miracles on occasion, but others have taken up the mantle and the Welsh winter Saturday retains its traditional flavour, each team doing battle for name and fame among the towns as it did in 1880. 'Who have we got today?' we say. We grit our teeth. We prepare for the fray. We might be nineteen or ninety, but the anticipation is the same, and whether we are snugged down in that peculiar sub-terranean enclosure with its worm's-eye view of the players at Llanelli, or perched high on the sculptured slopes of Pontypool Park, we are soon involved with our favourites. The most partisan amongst us have no time for the referee unless he offends or especially pleases us, and then

22
22

Some things are unchanging in all the hundred years of Welsh rugby: *Opposite page: above*, Police in concert during Swansea v. Springboks game in 1969; *below left and right*, And it hurts! Injuries for David Richards (Jerry Lewis, long-standing trainer, is in attendance) and Graham Price. *This page: left and below*, More injuries, for Stuart Lewis and Mark Keyworth

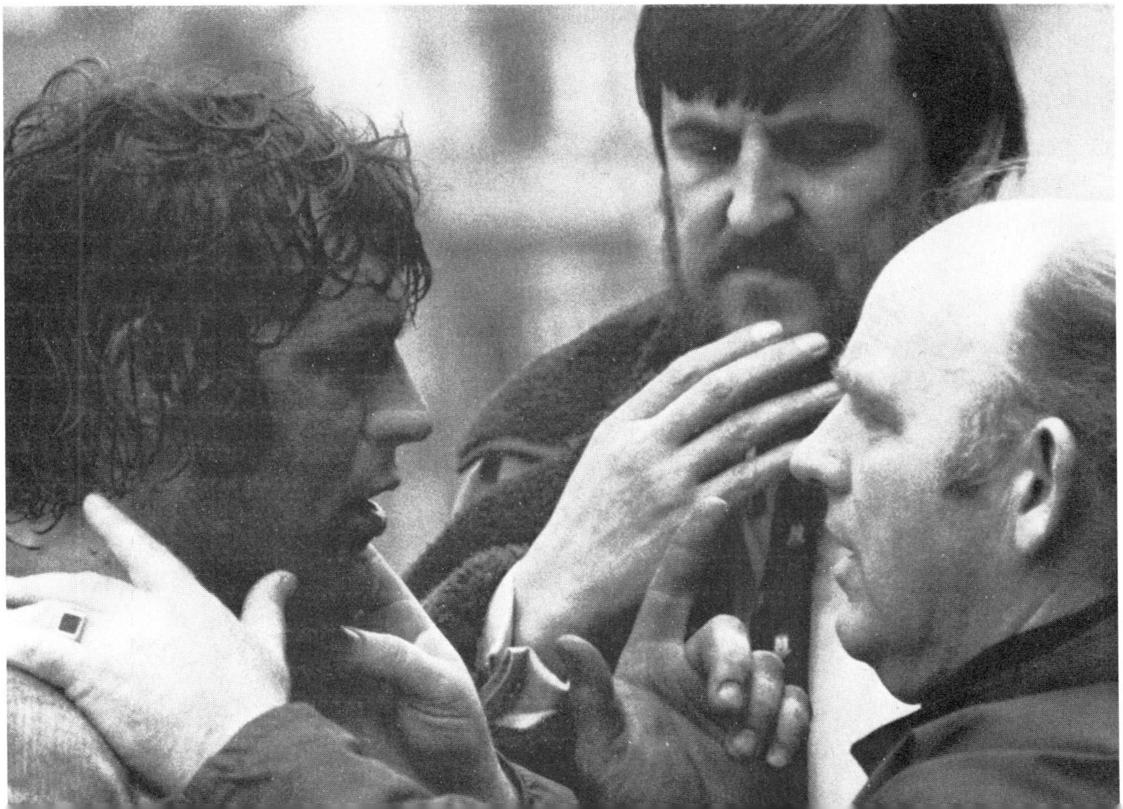

we are ever ready to advise him or his critics if we disagree with them. 'Go down and ask him for a loan of the whistle,' we suggest with glee to the insistent protestors. 'Ask him nicely, mind!' We think we see all, that omniscience is a part of our heritage. We are wrong, of course, but we feel we are part of the scheme of things and this is the nub of it. Welsh rugby football not only speaks for us and to us, but gives so many of us those twin essentials of fellowship, a sense of status and belonging, without which we would be a lesser and more anonymous people, dwarfed by the uniformity of a grey world.

Afterword by Carwyn James

It is proper that a writer should address himself to a centenary of Welsh rugby. It was Gwenallt in a poem called *Rygbi* who maintained that Yr Alltwen was not a village on the map of Wales, that the workers did not belong to any single country, that the proletariat knew no boundaries as they worshipped the flame at the head of the stack, the flame of world justice and the brotherhood of man.

Cultivating the garden, caring for the pig and the game on Saturday were some of the pleasures which made life bearable. Gwenallt goes on to say that all week they dreamt of the feast of the red jerseys coming face to face with the English at St Helen's, and how they used to get excited when Bancroft kicked a goal and Dicky Owen scored his try for Wales.

As an international arena St Helen's, Swansea, is no more. Another poet from the Swansea valley, Crwys, captured the mood of the big day at the Arms Park in Cardiff by referring to the trumpets blazing, the drums beating, *Sospan Fach*, the song of Stradey Park, Llanelli, sung like a hymn, a leek hanging on the upright and everyone being terribly, terribly Welsh.

The Reverend A. E. Jones, Cynan, was even more perceptive, perhaps daring, certainly a prophet. In 1932, competing for the Crown at the Royal National Eisteddfod, his inspiration was neither St Helen's nor the Arms Park but Twickenham. His subject was the crowd, the crowd that eventually willed Wales home to an arrogant victory, one year before it even happened, because for twenty years and two the Welsh couldn't lay the cabbage-patch bogey.

In January 1933, led by Watcyn Thomas, Llanelli born and Llanelli bred, they did. Vivian Jenkins and the young student from Rydal School, Wilfred Wooller, were awarded their first caps, Raymond Bark-Jones, a North Walian and the captain of Cambridge, was selected, and the army were persuaded to grant leave of absence to a Welsh-speaking Welshman called Vaughan Jones. The mix was so, the motivation mighty and the front-row was majestic.

In the seventies the cry 'Up-and-under here we go!' came from Charlie Faulkner, Bobby Windsor and Graham Price, the Pontypool front row; in 1933 the cry came from Llanelli. Bryn Evans propped by Edgar Jones and Archie Skym, a bulldog of a man and a policeman, were the equal of any. Within fifteen minutes Bryn had broken his nose, he refused to leave the field and for the rest of the game it bled like a tap and made the Twickenham grass greener. It also bled the bogey.

Two years later in 1935, both Swansea and Wales did to New Zealand what Gallaher's men had suffered in 1905; Tanner and Davies of Gowerton, schoolboy halves of Swansea, and Tanner and Cliff Jones for Wales. I saw Willie Davies playing; I regret not having seen Cliff Jones. 1905, 1935 and 1953 were vintage years with victories over the All Blacks. Since then, in a glittering golden era even better than the first at the turn of the century, Wales has lost on seven occasions to the South Island, both here in Wales and in New Zealand. In fact, since 1964 when Wales toured South Africa, we haven't travelled well. Our record abroad in the land of the springbok, the puma, the kiwi and the wallaby is not a good one. However, at home in Britain and in France in the seventies our record was second to none.

It is better now, so states the statistical evidence, than the original decade of domination inspired by the likes of Winfield, the Bancrofts, Owen and Trew, Percy Bush, Rhys Gabe an Gwyn Nicholls. It is also better than it was during the ten years when England was suffering from the broken-time controversy and the break-away of the clubs to play the professional thirteen-man rugby league game, and before France had been accepted into the championship fold.

There were seven defeats in forty-three matches in that era. But the modern record is now even better and, following the defeat of Rives' France at Cardiff in January 1980, Wales hadn't lost a championship match in twenty-three games since 1968, when the French beat us by five points. The points count to me is duller than the try count. Points can suggest the Big Bertha toe-kickers of the calibre of Jenkins or

Jarrett, or the round-the-corner finesse of Phil Bennett, or 'The King'.

John Billot, a thorough, reassuring researcher, reminds us that in the fray with the four nations during the last decade we scored ninety-one tries and had thirty-six scored against us, twenty-one more tries than France, forty-seven more than England. The first was scored by the Newport flyer Laurie David and the last by another wing, Elgan Rees, who just beat the substitute Clive Griffiths to the touch-down.

Griffiths had a few moments of glory as a replacement for J. P. R. Williams, the Welsh captain, against England in 1979 which reminded us all of the occasion five years previously when Willie Steele's Scottish boot has caused a depressed fracture of J. P. R.'s upper jaw. This in turn caused him to miss one of the most sensational tries of the seventies which was scored by Gareth Edwards, caked in mud, following a mad dash from a controlled kick and a chase.

The seventies belonged to these men: Williams' stoical courage, so contagious that kids at school these days want to be high-leaping, hari-kiri full-backs; the strength of the Nonconformist Gareth Edwards, long of pass, selective on the break, always independent, always himself. And Gareth reminds us of the chunky, cheeky chappie from Maesteg who came on as a replacement for him at Twickenham in 1970, twenty minutes to go, Wales losing, to score a vital winning try.

A year later for the Lions in the first test at Dunedin, Ray Hopkins again replaced Edwards after only six minutes of play, and speaking of his fly-half Barry John who won the game for the tourists, he said, 'Looked after him like a baby, didn't I!' And on another occasion he produced the same captivating humour that is so important in a tourist, and initially an overweight tourist: 'Boys, don't come too near me now. I'm so sharp, you'll cut yourselves!'

John Dawes' team of 1971, coached by the irrepressible Clive Rowlands, if not the best of the decade most certainly set the highest possible standards for all that followed. They won the first Grand Slam since 1952 when John Gwilliam had led Wales with a schoolmasterish discipline, the good sense of a practising Quaker and the confidence of Cambridge. These qualities were responsible for Welsh victories in the Triple Crowns and Grand Slams in 1950 and 1952.

The business of selection is a matter for the 'Big Five', but sometimes players seem to pick themselves. The selectors seen here were responsible for the team that began the most successful era of Welsh rugby ever in 1970/71. *left to right*: Jack Young, Clive Rowlands, Cliff Jones, Harry Bowcott and Rees Stephens

1969, too, was a vintage year until disaster struck in New Zealand with two test defeats during an ill-organised tour, but these setbacks put steel into players of calibre. The Welsh team of 1971 was the backbone of the Lions' successful team in New Zealand and on their return, though possibly tired, they still played an unbeaten season.

For me, the most memorable match that Wales played was on 27 March 1971, at Stade Colombes, our first win in Paris for fourteen years. Dauga, one of the great forwards in the Jean Prat—Spanghero mould, scored a try which the current Italian national coach, Pierre Villepreux, converted. Wales scored twice, A J.P.R. interception was backed up by Gareth Edwards although Denzil Williams would have been there had Gareth not made the line, then Jeff Young stole a tight head and it was Barry John's turn to score from the scrummage with the insouciant calm of a maestro at a master class.

John Dawes,
Coaching
Organiser,
WRU

When John Dawes made his post-match banqueting speech in French and in Welsh he received a standing ovation. Denzil Williams was heard to mutter that he hadn't understood a word and asked which language was spoken first, anyway! The men of Gwent may not speak the language but they have a strong awareness of being Welsh and, as Ray Prosser constantly reminds those of us living west of Loughor Bridge, 'We're responsible for keeping them English out, we live closer to them!'

It was in Wales' defeat of France that Barry John transgressed the ethics of the fly-half union when he actually tackled Dauga and for his sin broke his nose; thereafter he reverted to the finger-tip tackling for which the more discerning fly-halves are famous.

Not so the back-row boys, Dai Morris, Terry Cobner, John Taylor and Mervyn Davies. They tackled head on like tigers: there was Mervyn's superb tackle on Mark Loane of Australia, J.P.R.'s tackles on the likes of Gourdon of France and B. G. Williams of New Zealand, all the more classical beside the delicate approaches of J. J. Williams and Gerald Davies who were equally effective from the side.

It will be discussed, argued, pondered, how much of Wales' success in the seventies was due to the coaching explosion of the sixties which led to the appointment of Ray Williams and Malcolm Lewis, coaches of stature, and how much to the high-class quality of star players.

Dr Nathan Rocyn Jones, the President of the W.R.U., had this to say when he opened the Conference of Coaches at Bridgend on 6 December 1964: 'The Union has watched with some anxiety the course of our rugby over the last few years and now looks hopefully to the efforts of the Coaching Committee and our coaches.'

Unquestionably coaching did help. Its outstanding contribution has been a significant improvement in forward organisation. In the last decade, at all levels, every forward has learned his function in life, his own personal skills and his particular contribution to the forward unit in all phases of play. The modern forward is a bigger and faster specimen who has to learn the disciplines of his trade.

Norman Gale, Jeff Young and later Bobby Windsor were powerful scrummaging hookers; Barry Llewellyn, Denzil Williams, Charlie Faulkner and Graham Price were props in the same mould as Courtney Meredith and Billy (W.O.) Williams, highly acclaimed by the Springboks.

In the second row Wales were well served following the B. G. V. Price and Brian Thomas era by Delme Thomas, the gentle giant of Llanelli, the London Welshmen Geoff Evans and Mike Roberts, and latterly by Alan Martin and Geoff Wheel. Derek Quinnell graduated into a utility player of calibre, lock, flanker and number eight.

As number eight and a fine leader of men, Mervyn Davies dominated the seventies, bringing to the position his own expertise with its accent on ball-winning and a far tighter game than the traditional concept of the corner-flagging number eight.

Dai 'the Shadow' Morris was a tireless toiler whose ambition in life seemed to be a consuming desire to live in proximity to the ball. John Taylor was a superb footballer, highly intelligent, a strong fearless tackler and one of the best mid-field support players I ever saw. Under Ray Prosser's tuition and influence Terry Cobner developed into a top-class player and a leader of quality, latterly lending to Wales some of

left, 'R.H.'—his fame was such that his surname was unnecessary *right*, Derek Quinnell, Llanelli, Wales, Lions

Pontypool's skills at rucking and working the rolling maul.

There were other notable forwards well drilled by their club coaches and by the national coaches of the seventies, Clive Rowlands and John Dawes. And with the accent on winning quality possession, the backs also flourished. Both Gareth Edwards and Gerald Davies scored twenty tries for Wales, Gareth's half century of appearances was almost approached by J.P.R. and Gerald, Phil Bennett and then Steve Fenwick place-kicked as well as Barry John. All the records seemed to have been broken: personal appearances, points, Triple Crowns and Grand Slams.

The decade will also be remembered for the re-introduction of the Welsh Challenge Cup which has proved highly successful in bringing the top and the smaller clubs together; many heroic battles have been fought. Provided Welsh club rugby maintains its present high standard, Wales, under the guidance of its new coach John Lloyd, can enter the eighties with confidence.

Dai Morris, 'the Shadow', in attack

I trust that the verities will remain, however, and like Alun Richards I believe that the jewel in the Welsh crown has always been half-back play and, with it, an expression of that flair which comes from the presence of so many instinctive players. Most of us remember the Barbarians' first try against the Seventh All Blacks. I remember it not only for its technical skill in the arts of passing, or the excellent support work and continuity of its execution, but for its spirit, its challenge, the defiance of the opposition from a hopelessly defensive situation. I can see it now and the impression is indelible.

A rolling ball, still rolling away from the nearest player deep inside his own twenty-five; black shirts and shorts in hopeful pursuit, and Phil Bennett, the player much criticised for not taking on the opposition at the time, gathers confidently, declining to kick for touch as everyone expected him to do. Instead he turns, ignores the touchline, and with all the panache of a ten-year-old playing 'internationals' with the kids next door in his own back garden, he begins to weave a delightful incisive pattern—a triple sidestep off his right foot—and in that moment there occur the three acts of deception if you like, and a great try is born, setting the tone for the truly admirable game which was to follow. It was also the true spirit of rugby football, the rare and memorable moment when a player is playing at a level other than the conscious, the unique moment when the game almost assumes an art form.

Remembering this moment and others like it, I often ask myself why it is that we rarely see truly great performances from our mid-field players nowadays. I don't pretend to have the exact answer, but I have a theory that part of the reason lies in a decline in the status of the outside-half. Along the years we have produced excellent stand-off halves and, Chapel or Church, they usually look as if they are of Iberian extraction: on the small side, quick over short distances, speedy on the turn and quick thinking with lots of native cunning—a better word this than intelligence, for the best of them are given to playing much of their game by instinct. If you asked them to analyse their game they probably couldn't. These were the most pressurised players on the field, the players to be marked out of the game by opposing sinners because they were the pivots of attacking three-quarter lines. To stop the stand-off was to stop the whole side and the game of my youth gave every advantage to destructive wing-forwards.

Then came the changes in the off-side laws relating in particular to line-outs and scrums. At once the wing-forwards and other defenders were kept further away from the opposing halves and not as they were when I was playing in my first game for Llanelli against Pontypool. Then I was within shaking-hands-distance of such infidel destroyers as Ray Cale and Alan Forward whose hot breath I felt for most of the match! This was pressure of the most intense kind, but with the changes in the laws, the stand-off of today is under far less strain from the opposing flankers. It is our privilege as old-style players who learned in the heat to tease the moderns by telling them that anyone could play in the position these days.

Briefly, the changes in the laws meant a revolutionary alteration in the way a stand-off half plays his game, and whereas in my day we rarely planned moves beforehand and were reluctant to tell our centres what would be done if we gained possession, today the modern fly-half has more time to think, time even to make a conscious decision whether to run at the opposition or to pass. In this situation, particularly when set moves are frequently rehearsed, the instinctive half tends to play safe and to pass along the line. Indeed, if one of the centre three-quarters is in charge of the line, the stand-off is often given no option.

To counteract this, I would always give the stand-off the responsibility for calling the moves, to revert to his historical role, and in this context it is worth noting that the important quality in a scrum-half is quickness and accuracy. Neither Tanner nor Gareth Edwards gave ponderously long passes, it was the speed and timing which made them supreme. In Gareth Edwards' case, the exceptional length created a new opportunity for Barry John to invent a move of his own which would be rare in the old-fashioned game. Sometimes Barry John took Edwards' passes virtually standing still, but such was his confidence that he even paused and forced the opposition to run at him before he slipped them. He was, of course, a player of the transitional period with experience of the two eras of the game, and he also benefitted from touring with players of the calibre of Dawes and Mike Gibson who allowed him to be the pivot of the attack.

But to me, for all our appreciation of Welsh flair and the need to find room for its expression in modern patterns of play, there is no escaping basics, and there never has been. The most complex moves will only work provided the players can do the mechanics of the moves well; in other words, provided they can catch or pass accurately at top speed without wasting time or space. One of the secrets of Welsh success in the seventies was the presence in the line of players like John Dawes and Arthur Lewis who could give and take a pass in one stride. Watching them, there was nothing so satisfying as seeing the ball moving rapidly 'like molten lead', as Sir Wavell Wakefield used to say, and the famous victory against the Seventh All Blacks was achieved by the speed of passing as much as anything else, a speed that I saw repeated by a splendid Australian schoolboys' side against the Welsh Secondary Schools some years ago.

Doing the basics well, giving and taking the ball at speed is the essence of good three-quarter play, and, for all our recent pre-occupation with physical domination up front, the Welsh contribution to the game in any era is best expressed by Milton who summed it up: 'Who overcomes by force, hath overcome but half his foe.'

The fact of nationhood and nationality is transcended by such sentiments as Milton's, but this perceptive pictorial essay is about the Welsh and our love of rugby. Happily it takes a pride in our achievements and our contribution to the game. In everything it is true to the spirit of Gwenallt and his early poem on our national game *Rygbi*. This poem's message is also the same in essence, and it is a healthy reminder that you can only care for the nations of the world provided that, first and foremost, you learn to care for your own. Therein lies all the glory.

Index

Page numbers in *italic* refer to the illustrations